# ONCE UPON A CRISIS

## A LOOK AT POST-TRAUMATIC STRESS IN EMERGENCY SERVICES FROM THE INSIDE OUT

# WILLIAM MAY

MINDSTIR MEDIA

Published by Mindstir Media
PO Box 1681 | Hampton, New Hampshire 03843 | USA
1.800.767.0531 | www.mindstirmedia.com

Printed in the United States of America

ISBN-13: 978-0-9883162-0-1

Library of Congress Control Number: 2012949629

Visit William May on the World Wide Web:
www.crisisbook.net

# DEDICATION

*To the souls departed, those left behind,*
*and those who tried to make a difference.*

# TABLE OF CONTENTS

# OPENING STATEMENT

Townsend, Massachusetts is a rural New England postcard village, especially in the fall when the leaves on the deciduous trees turn brilliant reds, oranges, and yellows. When Mother Nature creates a firestorm of colors within her woodlands that poses no threat to anyone or anything, yet is so exciting to witness firsthand. Especially in the warm glow of a waning afternoon sun, when a slight breeze causes the foliage to flicker to and fro, making the forest appear on fire. In the winter when the town turns white from snow there exists a meaningful tranquility about the place. The transformation from one to the other takes a few weeks, but seems to happen overnight with the first snowfall. The Town Common, rectangular in shape with a wooden gazebo in the center, is inviting to both residents and visitors alike. Surrounded by three churches, there are moments on clear bright evenings during the winter holiday season when the Town Common becomes a living symbol of peace on earth. You can see it. You can feel it. You can imagine too, how wonderful our world would be if the harmony of this silence could be spread around our planet. Even in our present fast-paced realm of instant communications there are moments when Townsend, population just shy of nine thousand, can take you back to a time when life seemed to move much slower. Like it did sixty years ago when I grew up there. I was raised in Townsend and consider myself one of Townsend's most fortunate sons even though I poked fun at my parents, teachers, and police in my first book "Billy Boy," a somewhat humorous account of my youth. I was brought up in a strict religious home where respect was a way of life and not just a word in Webster's Dictionary immediately following the adjective resourceful. I was that, as well, back in my early days, trying to stay one step ahead of my parents, teachers, and the law. However I wasn't as clever as I should have been because I often found myself two steps behind and in trouble much of the time. Nothing legally formal, just being a royal pain in the neck during my teenage years. So I guess it came as a shock to some, especially to those who grew up with me, that I would become Chief of Police of my hometown during my adult years. My wavering boyhood was a great education in preparation for my future career as a police officer. I invented many of the excuses given to me now by young people to justify the trouble they found themselves in. I knew them all. I had been there. I had done those things. Little did these young offenders know I held a B.S. Degree in getting off the hook and I don't mean a Bachelor of Science Degree in Fishing. I'm talking about B.S. in its purest form, bullshit. In fact, I often knew better reasons than they did, and on occasion would suggest a better way to minimize the problem a young offender got caught up in. To the best of my knowledge I'm the only police officer to ever use this "good cop, better excuse" routine.

I started my career at the bottom in January 1973, as a patrol officer working the midnight shift. Although advancing up through the ranks was a consideration, my primary focus was on being able to react and perform at my very best in an arena where the unforeseen crisis required my immediate attention. Someone's life often depended on how well I did my job, as did the successful outcome of a criminal case. Unlike in the movies, frontline police work is done on the first take. Emergency service personnel most often only get one chance to get it right. They either make or break it, often in a matter of seconds, on their first and only time around. Within my first week on the job I knew I wasn't adequately prepared for the work I had chosen to do. I had been dispatched to a serious motor vehicle accident at two o'clock in the morning and found the lone occupant of the vehicle bleeding profusely from a head injury. I used first aid techniques I had learned in Boy Scouts years earlier to slow the bleeding until an ambulance arrived. As a result, I spent my first years on the job expanding my education. I received certification as an Emergency Medical Technician from the National Registry in June 1974, graduated from the Massachusetts State Police Municipal Officer Training Program in 1975, and their Crime Scene Search School in 1976. I earned an Associate of Science Degree in Criminal Justice from Mount Wachusett Community College and was at the top of my game by the summer of 1977. I advanced to the rank of Sergeant, was in excellent physical shape, and in my mind, felt there wasn't any emergency I couldn't successfully handle. In 1981 I was promoted to the top slot at the police department and served in that capacity until I retired in June 2002. During that timeframe most people acknowledged me as "Chief," while some older folks who knew me during my youth simply called me "Billy." Either way both names resonated with respect for the position I held. When someone referred to me as Billy however, I knew right away that I was dealing with a person who had known me for many years. Part of my success as a small town Police Chief was a direct result of this "Billy factor," my long-term connection with people in the town where I grew up. This provided me with an ability to put my finger on the daily pulse beat of my community. I knew who was related to who, I knew what was important, what was trivial, when to apply the law, and at what strength to apply it. My success was also a direct result of the people who worked alongside me, which consisted of a team of fifteen full-time officers, two secretaries, and twelve part-time officers. In 1990 the Town of Townsend built a new police station and emergency communications center, and I later became responsible for supervising this operation and the eight emergency communications specialists who made our emergency system work successfully.

The communications center received and directed all incoming calls to the appropriate agencies. Some were solely the responsibility of the police and communications center staff, but there were also calls that were fire department, fire department rescue, or ambulance priorities. In short, there were five teams playing the urgent situation game. Winning the game required that everyone worked together. Time of day, time of year made no difference. Emergencies never took a holiday. Some of the players volunteered their time or worked for minimal pay, doing their job simply to help others. To say I worked alongside good people would be an understatement. I worked with the very best. Humble, but well honed within their respective professions, these dedicated public servants answered the call that on occasion involved extreme risk to their own well-being. I would do an injustice to my own personal service to fail to mention these team players. Much of my success in the emergency arena was a direct result of these first responders. They were, and still are, special people. If not for the sadness that often came with the territory, I had what I considered the "dream job," playing on the "dream team" in the town where I grew up.

There aren't many professions where you can go from the absolute joy of assisting in the birth of a child to the overwhelming sadness of holding a dead one in your arms, all within a period of a few weeks. By occupation I was given lawful license to enter into the homes of families, often when not wanted but desperately needed, especially in matters involving domestic violence. When the angry faces of those involved were not representative of the happy ones seen in the family portraits that adorned the walls. Often there were hours of nothing to do but paperwork or routine patrol followed by moments of complete chaos that had to be brought under immediate control. Over time my dream job became a nightmare, one from which I didn't think I would awaken. This is my story, as bad as it was, as good as it was, it was what it was and I can't change it, although there are parts I wish I could. Not for me so much, but for the lives lost and those so gravely impacted. What you are about to read are literary snapshots taken by the mind of a small town cop. There are just a few of them. Not a full album, just enough to tell my story, enough to give you some insight into a very interesting profession. Some appeared on the front page of the newspaper while others would be lost forever if not

4

portrayed here. In some instances I use the actual names of the people involved, while in others I use fictitious first names only for obvious reasons. In an age of full disclosure I must warn you that some of what you are about to read won't be easy to mentally digest. You may find yourself going from feeling good on one page to welling up with tears on the next. That's just the way it was. The way I remember it. The way it will remain.

# CHAPTER 1

## BLACK ROCK
### SUMMER 1974

The only formal training I had received to assist me with my duties as a police officer going into the summer of 1974 was an emergency medical technician course I had pursued on my own, and completed in June that same year. Standardized police training had just been approved in Massachusetts and I was on a waiting list to attend the Massachusetts State Police Academy in Framingham. Most of what I knew with respect to criminal and motor vehicle law was taught to me on the job by older, some not necessarily wiser, officers. In addition, I had access to an entire library of the Massachusetts General Laws at the police station located in the basement of the Town Hall and would often consult them when required.

I had been working the night shift but had signed up for an additional "fill in" day shift on Thursday, July 18, 1974. Normally I worked alone with my nearest back-up unit in a neighboring town, the officer of which was also working alone. On this particular day I had a new volunteer reserve police officer named Erving Marshall Jr. riding with me in my marked police cruiser. Many of the north central towns in Massachusetts appointed reserve police officers that volunteered their time in exchange for learning the job. This also provided the host department with an ideal opportunity to get a good look at a perspective new officer during the early stages of their career and weed them out if necessary.

I grew up in Townsend and Black Rock was a well-known swimming hole located along the banks of the Squannacook River. Big Boulder would have been a better name instead of Black Rock, for the single stone formation was massive. Plus it was gray in color, not black. The roughly forty-foot diameter boulder stood out not only because of its immense size, but it was the only boulder in the area, surrounded by tons of clean, white sand. Somehow, millions of years ago, Mother Nature's glacial icepack delivered the massive rock to Townsend. Over time, as the water flowed around one side of it and washed the sand away, half of the boulder became fully exposed along the river's edge. The opposite side was left deeply embedded into the remaining steep embankment that provided a land bridge to the top of the boulder. The danger at the top was very obvious and no one fooled around up there. The rock was so large it provided shelter from the rain on the bottom that was exposed to the river. Overall, Black Rock was a fun place during the summer. A special place that lingers in your mind and only surfaces when thoughts wander back to those summer days when you were young and carefree. When only laughter filled the air. When a fun-filled July afternoon seemed liked it would never end. Little did I know that on this third Thursday of the month Black Rock would take on a whole new meaning for me, the young officer riding with me, and Officer James Hamel. All three of us had grown up in Townsend and had enjoyed the boyhood pleasures of Black Rock, albeit a generation apart. On this day Black Rock would bond the three of us as one, for on this day we would have to depend on each other to survive. On this day, death came knocking at our door, and the key to our survival was not trying to fool death in hopes it would go away, but to meet the Grim Reaper head on. Face to face, eyeball to eyeball, and deliver to him a message loud and clear, "We have no intention of going anywhere with you today!"

My workday had started like any other. Officer Marshall and I discussed patrol procedures and made a verbal agreement that neither one of us would give up our weapon for the other. We both had a clear understanding of the lesson taught a few years earlier when one California officer surrendered his weapon in exchange for the release of his partner who was being held at gunpoint by three armed robbery suspects. Both were shot to death by their own service weapons. I made certain my young ride-along officer knew what I expected of him while on patrol. Just before lunch we received a radio transmission from our communications center that a man named Carl had left his home in Ayer, Massachusetts, after leaving a suicide note. The broadcast advised the make and color of the vehicle he was last seen driving, as well as the license plate number. We were further advised that the man was white, age 33, and that he was most likely armed with a high-powered rifle. We were also made aware that the person we were looking for was an avid fisherman, who enjoyed fishing the Squannacook River, about seven miles of which flowed through Townsend. Based on the information received I decided to systematically check known fishing spots along the river starting in Townsend Harbor on the east end of town and work west from there.

Early in the afternoon, about halfway through the checking process, Officer Marshall and I arrived at Black Rock by foot after leaving our police cruiser parked just off Dudley Road. There was a cart road that ran into the area but it was rough and not suited for motor vehicle use. As we walked up an incline toward the rock, we both noticed the vehicle we were looking for directly in front of us. The make, color, and license plate all matched. I raised my left hand up to my face and pressed my index finger against my lips, a silent gesture indicating "quiet" to make certain neither of us spoke. We both drew our service weapons as we slowly approached the vehicle, Officer Marshall on one side, myself on the other. I expected to find the man slumped down and deceased as a result of a self-inflicted gunshot wound, most likely to the head. From a distance there were no visible signs that a traumatic suicide had taken place. The vehicle doors were closed and the windows were clear and intact. The other thing that struck me was how absolutely quiet it was. No birds singing, no traffic sounds off in the distance. Nothing. Looking into the passenger compartment proved that the person we were looking for was not inside. From my observations I assumed he was somewhere in our immediate area. There were no keys in the ignition.

Using hand signals I motioned to Officer Marshall to follow me, and we proceeded to walk back out of the area the same way we came in. At a point where I felt we were out of earshot from the vehicle I radioed our communications center and advised dispatch that we had located the wanted vehicle but not the man being sought, and that we were going to conduct a search of the immediate area in an attempt to find him. I then told Officer Marshall that I wanted both of us to go back to where the vehicle was parked and walk down a footpath that ran easterly from that point. I made it clear that all communication between us would be via hand signals, and that he was to stay at least twenty yards to my rear. I was concerned that if the person we were looking for were still alive he wouldn't be thinking sensibly. In his confused state of mind he could possibly misconceive our intent, especially after noticing our holstered weapons, and open fire upon us. If he did I didn't want to give him the opportunity to hit two easy targets standing side by side. I wanted to control the situation as best possible. I wanted to make sure that if any shots were fired the second one would come from us.

With a plan in place we proceeded back past the parked vehicle and onto the footpath. The sound of silence was overpowering. Even the usual rummaging squirrel was nowhere to be seen. The haunting absence of normal sound and movement in the forest was obvious. Something was wrong. Even nature's little creatures knew it. The warning signs were all around us. As I rounded a corner in the path the silence was broken when the man we were looking for noticed me at the exact same time I noticed him. He was sitting cross-legged on the ground about twenty yards ahead of me, a long-barrel rifle resting across his legs, his back resting against a large oak tree. He started to raise the rifle in my direction and I yelled to him, "Carl, stop, put the gun down, don't make me shoot you!" as I drew my service weapon and pointed it at him. He held the rifle pointed down and yelled back, "Go ahead and shoot me, that's what I came here for!" Officer Marshall took cover behind a large tree to my rear and I slowly took cover behind a tree closest to me. The man just sat there, gun in hand. I didn't know if the gun was loaded, but based on the circumstances, assumed it was. I knew his intent was real and imminent so I yelled at him again, "Look Carl, put the gun down so we can talk about this. Please, at least for the moment, put the gun down." With that he set the gun back across his legs as he continued to sit cross-legged against the tree. Now I had to stretch the moment I just gained into minutes, hopefully hours. I noticed approximately six beer cans on the ground in front of Carl and that he was smoking a cigarette. I didn't know how much alcohol he had consumed or how much he had left. Was he still heading up or coming down mentally from the beer? Were any of the cans still full? The same held true for the cigarettes. What happens when he runs out of tobacco? Alcohol? Thus began a long afternoon of trying to persuade a mentally disturbed person to stop what he was doing and surrender his weapon.

Officer Marshall and I held our positions and I radioed for back-up units, making it clear that responding units were not to use sirens. I didn't want Carl to know that more of us were coming, and I was concerned that the sound of a siren would set him off. All he had to do was raise the gun to his chest or head and pull the trigger. I was too far from him to prevent this from happening but knew I had to take control of the weapon at some point, the sooner the better. The best thing we had going for us, all three of us, was we were talking to one another. I knew we had to keep this up. I'd talk to him for a while and when our conversation grew stale Officer Marshall would start a new line of verbal communication. From the distance that separated us I knew there was no way I could stop the guy from doing what he came to do, but there were things I could do to slow the process down. As long as he was talking his mind was being distracted from his thoughts of self-destruction, his mental focus directed toward us and not solely on himself. If we could keep him talking maybe we could slow the whole thing down and bring it to a stop. Maybe he'd surrender the weapon. Maybe he'd fall asleep. All I needed were a few seconds to take full control of his weapon. There were unknowns that bothered me, however. What led him to conclude that killing himself was the only way out? How much alcohol had he consumed?

How much sleep had he had within the last twenty-four hours? My biggest concern, he wanted to die and I didn't. How much risk should I take to save his life?

Officer Jim Hamel, who was off duty, had stopped by the police station and heard my call for "additional units." As a result he jumped into a police car coming from a neighboring community and came to our location. I continued to hold my position and via handheld radio set up a strategic staging area about a quarter mile from where Officer Marshall and I were located. We continued to talk to Carl without taking a break in between. While Officer Marshall talked to him, I used my hand-held radio to learn all that I could about Carl. I learned he was married, had a daughter, his parents were alive, he had a brother that lived in a neighboring town, and that he was a Catholic who attended church weekly. As a result I requested back-up units pick up Carl's brother and the local Catholic priest and bring them both to the staging area. I further requested that an ambulance crew be sent to our area, for one way or the other, I knew for certain Carl would be leaving with us. I just didn't know in what condition he would be in when we departed. I continued to talk to Carl in an attempt to slow things down. I had control over everything except the rifle that he kept resting across his legs, and from what I could see, his right hand was in the location of the trigger. I tried to reason with him by explaining I didn't know what led him to where he was, but whatever it was could be corrected. No matter what I suggested he kept telling me I didn't understand. Ironically he was right, I didn't understand. What was so disturbing in this man's world that led him to the point that he wanted to end his life? With a high-powered rifle no less. I kept thinking that if he started to raise the rifle I would attempt to stop him by firing an accurately placed non-lethal shot to his lower body, and perhaps save his life. How ironic; shoot someone to save their life? The afternoon dragged on. From a point where Carl could hear but not see, we had the local parish priest try to talk Carl into putting the rifle down. His words were not convincing enough and the standoff continued. Supper hour was upon us and I asked Carl if he was hungry, hoping to gain close access to him by delivering some food. Carl was intoxicated perhaps but not hungry, refusing my offer of food. I then tried having his brother talk to him. Carl was shocked to hear his brother's voice. He sat right up when he first heard him. After initial contact they yelled back and forth to each other, not as a result of anger, but because of the distance their voices were required to travel. They talked about their boyhood, their lives, and I felt maybe we were making progress. As the conversation continued, however, Carl started to get angry with his brother and I jumped back into the banter to calm the situation back down.

The setting sun was starting to cast long shadows as it started to slide from the sky. Time was running out. I had less than two hours of daylight to work with before the sun went down. I knew the forest was about to get extremely dark which would only compound the problem I was trying to solve. A depressed man armed with a rifle under the influence of alcohol equates to trouble. Throw darkness into the equation and the situation escalates to a crisis of unmanageable proportion. I had successfully controlled Carl up to this point through verbal communication and had occasional one to one visual contact. The unknown that darkness was about to bestow upon us would change that. I wouldn't be able to see what he was doing. The standoff had to be brought to an end. I had to take control of his rifle.

I had been sizing up Carl from the beginning. He was of average build and about my age. I hadn't seen any action with respect to beer so I figured he was coming down from the alcohol. He hadn't eaten since we first made contact, either. Hopefully this was making him tired, perhaps weaker to a certain extent. I knew that no matter what was said to Carl, or who said it, the gun was going to remain under his control. The moment had come to take aggressive action.

I huddled with Officers Marshall and Hamel to go over a new plan to force the issue and bring it to conclusion. Officer Hamel was to use the department bullhorn and keep talking to Carl. Officer Marshall was to engage verbally with Carl, but his primary function was to shoot him if he became a threat to any of us. Of extreme importance was to keep Carl talking. Keep him distracted. Keep making noise; lots of noise. My job was to sneak around through the woods to the rear of the large oak tree that Carl was sitting against and forcibly take control of the rifle. Upon my hand signal, Officer Marshall was to get angry with Carl, yell at him, and start throwing leaves and branches forcibly down onto the ground to create a major diversion. At this precise moment I would make my move. With only minutes of daylight remaining the plan was set in motion.

I took off my clothes from the waist up to shed myself of any shiny objects, such as buttons or badges, to prevent any movement I made from being reflected by the setting sun. Fifteen minutes had passed by the time I successfully made my way undetected to the rear of the tree that Carl was sitting up against. I could see a portion of the back of Carl's head on the left side of the tree. He appeared to be looking downward toward the direction of Officer Hamel's voice. I peeked around the right side of the tree for a few seconds to survey the weapon. The rifle was a bolt action, the breech was closed, and it was pointing downward to Carl's left as it rested across his legs. He did not have his right trigger finger inside the trigger guard, which was a good thing. I could not see the gun's safety action. For what I was about to attempt I considered the safety to be off and the gun to be loaded. I went over in my mind what I was about to do one last time, knowing that I had to be fast, and then gave Officer Marshall the hand signal to put our plan into action. With that Officer Marshall started his rant and threw some branches on the ground, while Officer Hamel started yelling at him over the bullhorn. I made my move. I completely surprised Carl as I came into his view from the right side of the tree. He started to stand up. I grabbed the barrel of the rifle with my left hand and the rifle proper just rear of the trigger guard with my right. In an instant Carl was standing, the rifle barrel now between our heads. Carl slipped his trigger finger inside the trigger guard and pulled. The rifle fired a deafening blast. I felt the rush of air being sucked away and the heat from the muzzle as the bullet discharged from the weapon between our heads. In an instant I gained control of the weapon with both hands and kneed Carl in the groin as I turned into him. As he fell forward toward me I swung the butt of the rifle up across his face. He fell to the ground in pain. My ears were ringing. The standoff was over.

# AFTERMATH:

The ambulance crew came in and removed Carl to the hospital. On the ground in front of where Carl was sitting were some empty beer cans and many cigarette butts. In the middle of the mess was a photo of a woman and a young girl along with a handwritten note in which Carl apologized to his family for taking his own life. I took possession of the note and photograph and cleared the scene. Later that evening I was advised that I had broken Carl's jaw. I also found out that Carl worked for a bank outside of my jurisdiction that had just discovered he had embezzled six thousand dollars. As time passed I went on to other cases and Carl drifted to and from my mind.

Three years after that summer day I received a letter in the mail from Carl. He told me how he stole the money from the bank and that he had paid the money back as part of a plea deal with the court and the bank to avoid jail time. The picture that I retrieved on that terrible day was that of his wife and daughter. He advised that he was back with his family, living with them in Florida, and how much he loved them. He explained he had every intention of shooting himself and would have if I hadn't intervened. Not because of the criminal consequences he faced by stealing the money, but because of the embarrassment he had caused for his wife, daughter, and family. In conclusion he thanked me for saving his life.

Although I took the lead role in this matter, many people contributed to preventing Carl from taking his life. Police work is much like other professions in the sense that teamwork is fundamental to success. Officer Marshall became Chief of the Townsend Police Department in 2002 after I retired. Officer Hamel entered the state policing system and became Chief of the Fitchburg University Campus Police Department in 2005. We remain close friends. I never heard from Carl again.

# CHAPTER 2

# AUTUMN LEAVES
## FALL 1975

By the fall of 1975 I had been working the four to midnight shift for almost three years. About six o'clock one late November evening I received a radio call advising me to meet a man at the phone booth next to the Old Brick Store in West Townsend. I was advised that the man had lost his wallet and was requesting assistance. Darkness comes early in November in Townsend. With clouds obscuring any sign of the fingernail moon in the sky, shadows were dimmed to almost nonexistence. I arrived within a couple of minutes to find an elderly man standing next to the telephone booth. The booth was made of aluminum, encased in glass on three sides with a two-panel accordion-fold glass door. Inside the booth next to the pay telephone was an aluminum shelf and an attached telephone book. Fall foliage season had passed, the trees in the area just skeletons of what they once were just a few weeks before, their red leaves turned brown, shed, and raked by the wind into scattered piles across the ground. I noticed when I arrived that there were two vehicles parked just across the street in front of Christian's Coffee Shop as well as a couple in front of the Brick Store. From a police perspective everything appeared normal with the exception of this gray-haired man. Not because of his age or dress, just that I had never seen him before.

I got out of my police cruiser and walked over to the elderly man by the phone booth. He was dressed for the cold evening that surrounded us. I learned that he was from Boston and had lived there all his life. He had driven west along Route 119 to get a last look at the beautiful fall foliage only to find most of the leaves had fallen. He was what folks in town called a "leaf peeper." He told me that he was disappointed that there wasn't much to see after such a long ride. He continued to tell me that he had stopped at the phone booth to call his wife to tell her that he was running a little late. He had taken his wallet out of his pocket, which he described as "black leather," and set it on the shelf inside the phone booth while making his telephone call. After speaking with his wife he then got back into his car and drove off. When he reached the traffic lights in the center of Townsend, a few miles down the road, he realized he had forgotten his wallet at the phone booth. He returned to find his wallet was not where he had left it and was truly disappointed. He doubted any money would be left in the wallet if we found it, but was concerned for other items of value contained inside, especially his driver's license. I felt bad for the guy and went back to my police cruiser to get a flashlight to start checking the area around the phone booth. Maybe with some luck we'd find something.

Just as I got to my cruiser I heard a fire tone come over my police radio followed by a verbal message regarding a fire in town. The location of the fire was at Christian's Coffee Shop; right across the street! I told the elderly man that I'd be right back and quickly walked to the coffee shop, which showed no visible sign of fire. I radioed, "Nothing showing on the outside" to my communications center and walked into the restaurant to find smoke hanging in the air. A small grease fire in the deep-fat fryer had set off the automatic fire alarm but the fire had been extinguished by the automatic fire suppression system overhead. As a result, four fire trucks and an ambulance arrived on the scene along with a contingent of volunteer firefighters and emergency medical people. The usual crowd of onlookers gathered to see what was going on as the cool November evening soon warmed up from excitement, not fire. I chatted briefly with three firefighters, made sure traffic was flowing properly, and returned to the elderly man patiently waiting near his car. I walked with him, my flashlight illuminating the ground as we shuffled back to the phone booth, kicking fallen leaves aside in a vain attempt to find his wallet.

People that had come out of their homes to see what was going on joined in to help find the wallet, too. The foliage on the ground made crunching sounds as we walked around and searched the area. If someone had taken the wallet, removed any money inside, and thrown it aside, it would be difficult to find among the groundcover of leaves. We were looking for a needle in a haystack.

As the two of us searched together I received a radio transmission advising me to see the Fire Chief who was standing across the street. I excused myself again and told the elderly man that I would be right back. I walked across the street to where the chief was standing. He handed me a black leather wallet and told me one of his firefighters found it lying along the side of the road just beyond one of his trucks. I opened the wallet and the name and address on the driver's license matched the elderly man I was assisting. I thanked the chief and walked back over to the saddened elderly man who was about to become very happy.

I walked up to him and said, "I've got good news for you. We found your wallet." He looked at me in disbelief until I held out his wallet. He took it in hand and opened it up to find all his money inside along with his driver's license and other personal documents. I could see his eyes starting to water up as he thanked me for finding his wallet. Then he said, "You know, I've heard stories about how people in small towns take care of others in need. How they look out for one another. I never expected so many would show up to help me find my wallet. I don't even live here and look at all the people who came out to help. This would never have happened in the city. I can't believe it. I just can't believe it." "Well," I said, "I'm just happy we could help you get your wallet back." He shook my hand; tears now coming down both cheeks, got back into his car and drove off. As best I could determine, the man for some reason put his wallet on the fender of his car and not on the shelf inside the phone booth where he originally thought. That would explain why a firefighter found the wallet on the edge of the road about three hundred feet east of the phone booth.

# AFTERMATH:

I was deeply taken by this elderly man's comments when I returned his wallet to him. I didn't want to spoil his wonderful impression of my hometown even though I knew he was mistaken by the activity he saw. Although falsely convinced, he was so right in this thinking. What he saw that night was a group of men and women who gave of themselves to protect others. Individual acts of kindness without any expectation of a thank you. I never heard from, or saw the man again. This incident happened almost thirty-seven years ago, and although Townsend moves at a faster pace now, the people who live there have not changed at all. They are honest and caring folk who give readily of themselves for others in need. The people in emergency services there haven't changed either. Sure there are some new faces that have replaced some old ones, but the tradition lives on, passed down from one generation to next. They are willing to lay it all on the line, including risking their own lives to help someone else. Even strangers. That's what people working in emergency services are all about.

# CHAPTER 3

# SPECIAL DELIVERY
## WINTER 1976

The four to midnight shift on Mach 18, 1976 started out like most all the others; quiet. I was the command sergeant over two other police officers, Officer Norman Johnson and Reserve Officer Bill Rousseau. On this night there would be two police cars patrolling the town. Johnson and Rousseau assigned to Car #41 while I worked out of Car #42. After reviewing the daily log from the day shift we set out on our separate patrols. The town was divided into four sectors. Sectors one and four on the west side, with two and three on the east. The operation was known as "splitting sectors," and would vary from day to day. Unusual for March, the temperature outside had plummeted down around zero degrees Fahrenheit, so there weren't many other vehicles seen out and about. The few that did pass by trailed long plumes of exhaust that normally wasn't visible on warmer nights. The cold could even be heard by the groaning of tires as they slowly moved around corners on the snowy frozen roadway. A rhapsody of asphalt agony, resonating in low-pitched rubbing sounds that only rubber can produce when being bitten by extremely cold pavement. From the outset I figured the next eight hours were going to be long and tiresome, so I settled in behind the wheel and drove along, the heater blowing full blast.

The shift seemed to drag on. I had worked quiet shifts before but the cold confining me to my police cruiser just made matters worse. There wasn't even any normal police activity to be heard over the police radio from other departments sharing our regional frequency. Nothing was happening. I started to think about the positive impact of not receiving any calls, which translated into not having to write any reports at the end of my shift. So as bad as the cold was, the quiet it brought with it was proving to be a good thing. Midway through the shift my police radio came blasting to life when our emergency telecomunicator radioed, "Car #41 and Car #42, immediate response is requested at 14 Squannacook Terrace, the MacMaster residence for a woman in labor." Talk about a wake up call! I knew Bob MacMaster very well. We grew up together. He was one year behind me during our grammar school years. I heard my companions in Car #41 radio that they had received the call and were responding. I radioed my dispatcher and advised I was doing the same and requested that an ambulance be dispatched as well. Although the three of us were trained in first aid, I was the only certified emergency technician on duty. I was about two minutes away from the MacMaster home when I started my immediate response and lit up my blue lights. There wasn't any traffic but department emergency vehicle response policy demanded my blue lights be flashing. My adrenaline started to rise. I started to go over childbirth procedures in my mind while racing to the scene. Everything I had been taught came flooding forth; cradle the head, remember newborns are slippery, suction the mouth, maintain an open airway, keep the newborn warm, tie off the umbilical cord, even with a shoe lace if necessary, monitor the mother, and so forth and so on. I had been well-trained to play in the big league of emergency childbirth but for some reason felt I'd never get into the game. Now this! Without warning I was being asked to step up to the plate. Finally after all those hours of recertification I was getting a chance to show how well I could do. Perhaps hit a home run, or maybe a grand slam if there were twins or triplets on the way. I was ready.

I arrived right behind Johnson and Rousseau, grabbed my emergency jump kit, and ran into the house. I went right into a downstairs bedroom to find Marcia MacMaster, Bob's wife, in intense labor. Birth was imminent. Bob was a nervous wreck, very concerned, and didn't know what to do. I knew the best thing to do was to get him out of the bedroom and keep him busy, so I told him to go boil some water in the kitchen. I was never trained to boil water in emergency childbirth situations, but I had seen it in the movies a couple of times. Bob must have seen the same movies because he immediately went to the kitchen to fulfill his role in the delivery. While Bob was in the kitchen the newborn arrived like babies have for centuries before. He was a boy who appeared cyanotic at first, then came the cry, followed by better skin color. Marcia was doing fine for the ordeal she had just gone through, too. Reserve Officer Monica Westerback, a nurse by profession, arrived with the ambulance and we tied off the umbilical cord. The baby was then wrapped in a blanket and placed in a laundry basket. Marcia was wrapped in a warm coat and along with her new son, taken to the hospital. I felt good about witnessing the greatest event known to humankind, the birth of a child. In this case the arrival of David MacMaster, age "brand new!" The Townsend Times ran a lengthy newspaper article about the event. I was the first emergency medical technician to deliver a baby in Townsend and got front-page press coverage. Of course, I didn't deliver the baby, Marcia MacMaster did. She did all the work and I got all the glory. I didn't have much to do with the whole thing really. Never got a chance to hit a home run as I had hoped. Never even had the opportunity to step up to the plate. I played defense instead, behind the plate, in the lowly role of catcher. Marcia was the one who went to the plate. She was the one that hit the home run. What I did didn't make much difference really. As long as Marcia was in the game, David would have arrived regardless of who else was on the playing field, including me.

# AFTERMATH:

I had a front row seat watching David grow up in Townsend. Just one of hundreds of nice kids I had the pleasure of observing mature from a distance. I would on occasion see David with his parents at various functions, or about town doing the things that boys headed toward manhood do. I saw him at police-sponsored programs, as well as safety talks at school. With the exception of a casual greeting now and then I didn't see David to talk to. A little over eighteen years would pass before I had a chance to have a lengthy conversation with him.

During the spring of every year, when the weather started to turn warm, I would park my unmarked police cruiser facing south along a half-mile straight section of Wallace Hill Road. The roadway led north away from the high school and was a quick way to go around the slower school bus traffic in the center of town. I would intentionally sit there just as school was getting out and do radar. I would compare what I did much to a grizzly bear catching salmon during spawning season. Just sit, wait a few seconds, and sure enough there would be another one. For the bear it would be another fish, for me another young speeding motorist. New drivers, especially young males, seem to have a need to drive fast during those first few days of warm weather before summer officially hit. I don't know why. I know I went through the same development crisis when I grew up in Townsend. Like the excitement found by a yearling in the pasture, teenagers like to kick up their heels when summer comes calling. This right of passage is wonderful to watch if the heel kicking happens in a field somewhere, when the only things that can make them go faster are their own two feet. When a couple hundred horsepower drives their acceleration the picture changes dramatically. I had delivered too many traffic death notifications to parents. I had also administered emergency care at crash sites and knew firsthand the pain that automobile accidents cause, both during as well as long after the accident was over. In an attempt to prevent as much sorrow as possible, I did my "radar thing" up behind the high school. I preyed upon good kids, from good homes. Not all, just the ones who for reasons that have eluded medical science since the advent of the automobile, develop heavy right feet when warm weather rolls around.

I nicknamed the Wallace Hill Road location the "Final Approach" as it was the last long straightaway to Townsend Center. I recorded motor vehicle speeds equivalent to those required for small aircraft on final approach to Logan International Airport, thus the special name given. Although some of the offenders were well over the posted speed limit I never wrote a traffic ticket for the many young "pilots" I stopped on final approach. I was trained how to write traffic citations at the Massachusetts State Police Academy. I was also trained in great detail about the impact of not writing one by Howard Doran, Chief of Police when I was seventeen years old and growing up in Townsend. He stopped me one night and instead of writing a traffic ticket called my father. I lost my license for a month. My father took it. Put it in his wallet. I didn't know until that sad moment in my life that my father was also the Massachusetts "Parental" Registrar of Motor Vehicles. Not for the entire Commonwealth of Massachusetts, just for the May family living on Main Street. My case was just the opposite of how the judicial system worked. I had no right to face my accuser, no right to cross-examine the witness against me, and no right of appeal for a matter in which I was found guilty before being afforded the opportunity to prove my innocence, which would have been a waste of effort anyway because I was guilty. I was going too fast. Case closed. License put into wallet. Not mine, my father's.

I guess you could say I applied the Chief Howard Doran proven method for traffic speed reduction along Wallace Hill Road behind the high school. However I changed the "Doran Method" and created a two-pronged double option approach to the problem. "Option A," write the ticket along with a heavy monetary fine, or "Option B," have your mother or father call me within twenty-four hours, and if they don't call me I'll send you the ticket in the mail. I felt this second option put the responsibility directly where it belonged. On only a few occasions was I forced to send the traffic ticket, and I had stopped hundreds of kids over the years. I found justice was better served at the hands of parents rather than the legal system when it came to young offenders of minor traffic violations. Less paperwork for me, less work for the courts, better results from parents, and seldom a second offense. In short, a better bang for the buck without spending the buck in the first place.

I was sitting along the "final approach" doing radar one warm May afternoon in 1993 when a vehicle approached me traveling over the posted limit. I activated my blue lights hidden in the grille of my unmarked police cruiser and the vehicle pulled over and stopped. As I approached the vehicle I noticed the operator was a young male. Why wasn't I surprised? I walked up and asked the operator for his license and registration. He appeared nervous as he handed me both. I read the name on his license: David MacMaster. The same David MacMaster that Marcia had delivered on a cold night so long ago. The same special delivery I "assisted" with behind the plate. I looked at David behind the wheel and said, "Good afternoon David. Do you remember me?" "To be honest Chief May," he said, "I don't remember when I was born, but I've heard the story at least a hundred times so I feel like I was there." Talk about an honest answer! Our meeting was cordial, at least from my perspective. I doubt David felt we were having a friendly chat especially after I gave him his choice of options. He did like most others and selected "Option B," the same one I would have picked under the circumstances. That evening I received a telephone call from David's father Bob, known around the MacMaster home as the "Parental Registrar of Motor Vehicles." I didn't see David drive by me for a few weeks after school got dismissed. Must have taken the bus home.

I would go on to "help" deliver two more babies in my career. Ironically both were boys, who like David, decided the best time to arrive on earth was on a cold winter night. Marcia and Bob MacMaster still live in Townsend where they raised their two boys. Nice kids from a good home. David furthered his education and graduated from Harvard. He now manages a team of investment brokers. He is married and has two children of his own. I expect in a few more years he'll take over the role his father once played in his life and become the MacMaster Parental Registrar of Motor Vehicles for his family. In a recent conversation David told me he remembered the day I stopped him on his "final approach" after school. He recalled being very nervous because he knew me as an "urban legend" back then. Urban Legend! I like that title better than Chief of Police!

# CHAPTER 4

## MIRACLE ON SMITH STREET
### SPRING 1978

I had been on the job for a little over five years. I had spent my first four years furthering my education in criminal justice and emergency medicine, and had grown confident in the work I was doing. In May of 1978 I was working a patrol shift and received a radio transmission to rapidly respond to 11 Smith Street for a child that wasn't breathing. I acknowledged my emergency communications operator and advised that I was "approximately a minute out," or about a minute away from the home. With that I activated my blue lights, siren, and responded to the call for help. I knew the address 11 Smith because Bill Barrett and his family lived there. Bill and I had grown up together.

During my response I went over the protocol for a non-responsive child. Absence of respiration regardless of age is life threatening. I also requested an emergency medical crew be dispatched to assist and was pleased to learn my emergency telecommunicator had already done this. Time was critical. I knew I only had four minutes at the very best before lack of oxygen to the brain would cause biological death. The vehicle I was driving was really moving, as was my thought process. During my rapid response I wondered why the child had stopped breathing. What could have caused this to happen? Could this be another case of Sudden Infant Death Syndrome? I had responded to a few S.I.D.S. emergencies, all of which ended tragically. I knew I was headed into a serious situation and could feel my training kicking in. I wanted to get there and get there fast. I didn't care what was waiting for me. I was up for the task. I was ready.

I pulled into the driveway at 11 Smith, grabbed my emergency medical jump kit from the front seat, and ran into the house. Christine Barrett, Bill's wife, met me in the doorway. She was crying and holding a lifeless baby girl in her arms. The child was cyanotic and appeared to be clinically dead. I took the child from her mother's arms and cradled her in mine, my left hand wrapped around the back of the child's head, her body resting face up along the inside of my lower left arm, her legs and feet extended beyond my left elbow on each side. I had practiced this with a "dummy" baby many times during training, but this was different. I knew I wouldn't be putting the dummy back in the storage box after this was over. If I failed, I'd be putting the child in a casket instead. This was the real deal. I looked and could clearly see there was no up and down respiratory movement in the chest area. I felt for a pulse with my right hand on the baby's brachial artery and there was nothing. I listened for a moment with my ear next to her mouth and heard nothing. I felt nothing. There was no warmth coming from her lungs. Her heart had stopped beating and she clearly wasn't breathing. I was holding the baby daughter of a friend in my arms and she was clinically dead. My reaction was immediate.

Placing my mouth over the baby's while pinching her nose shut, I immediately blew two small breaths of air into the child's mouth. As I started performing two-finger chest compressions on her heart the girl in my arms started to fuss. She quickly went from fuss to a full cry. Her skin color started to change from bluish gray to a more normal skin tone. Christine started to cry even harder than she had when I first arrived. Tears started coming down my cheeks as well. All three of us were crying when the ambulance crew arrived at the house to take Mom and daughter to the hospital.

# AFTERMATH:

The baby in my arms that day was Becky Barrett. Becky is now thirty-three years old and has two children of her own. Although many years have gone by I still recall that day on Smith Street as if it were just yesterday. Recently a pickup truck stopped alongside me while I was on one of my daily three-mile walks and the driver was Bill Barrett, Becky's father. We hadn't seen each other for some time. He introduced me to the person he was with by saying, "This is the guy that saved my daughter's life." We chatted for a few minutes before he continued on his way.

I was paid well for thirty years for the job I did. I was also given a bonus from time to time, but it wasn't included in my paycheck. Bonuses came my way in the form of happy endings. Becky Barrett was, and continues to be, a bonus far exceeding any monetary value. I recently spoke with Becky on the telephone and as we were saying goodbye she said, "Thank you for saving my life." I don't know about the rewards offered in other professions but I have been receiving the "Becky Bonus" for thirty-four years now. I have every reason to believe I will go on receiving it for the rest of my life. The real nice thing about it, I get it whenever I want. I just reach inside my mind and take it out to spend freely on another feel good moment. Life just doesn't get any better.

# CHAPTER 5

## SEAN COFFEY
### SPRING 1979

Sean Coffey was an energetic 10-year-old boy with sandy-blonde hair, freckles, and big brown eyes. The oldest of John and Nancy Coffey's four children, Sean was happiest when he was exploring near or far from his family's Townsend Hill farm on his Huffy bike, looking for a pickup football game or an adventure yet unknown. He was at an age of youthful discovery, and for Sean the "getting there" of the journey was just as exciting as the "happening" that awaited him on the other end. He had a ready smile, an adventurous spirit, and many friends. He roamed his Townsend Hill countryside, a rural area where time had slowly kept pace alongside the scattered families that had lived there for generations. A quiet setting dotted with farms, rolling fields, and beautiful mountain views, where neighborhood parents looked out for the children living in the area. This mutual caring for one another brought with it a feeling of safety that assured those living there that their peaceful coexistence could not be taken away. Sadly, this sense of security abandoned the Coffey's during the spring of 1979.

One afternoon in April of 1979 while John Coffey was driving home after work he noticed a large plume of smoke off in the distance coming from Townsend Hill and knew immediately that either his home or barn was on fire. He raced to the scene to discover his family safe, and together they watched as their home went up in smoke. The fire forced the Coffey's to move into a rental home on South Street, on the opposite side of the community, in an area known as Townsend Harbor; a busier part of town.

Townsend Harbor was named after a home located there that was once used as a stopping point for southern slaves fleeing north during the mid-1800s. With the aid of white sympathizers, black people who made this long and difficult journey in search of freedom, traveled along what history would record as the "Underground Railroad." A small pond next to this home became known as the Harbor Pond for this same reason. The name is deceiving in the sense one would think Townsend Harbor provided a safe haven for boats from the vicious throws of Mother Nature when in fact the need to protect man from the indignity of fellow man was what really gave it the name. There were only a few rowboats on the Harbor Pond when freed slaves passed through over 150 years ago, just as there were when John Coffey relocated his family there in the spring of 1979. Although the pond hadn't changed much over time, the area had. Unlike the constant tranquility that existed for generations upon the water, the pace of life around the pond during the late 1970s had quickened. People were moving in greater numbers, at much faster speeds.

With the exception of heavy periods of rain that caused the water to rise, the Squannacook River slowly zigzagged easterly through Townsend for approximately seven miles before emptying into the Harbor Pond, the water continuing on, eventually cascading over a waterfall at the eastern end. Fishing was common in the area and many an angler would spend hours trying to catch a few fish along the river or around the pond. Kids were drawn to it as well, as if they were the reincarnation of Tom Sawyer and Huckleberry Finn. Many people went fishing as a family, some packing lunches and making a day of it. Fishing was fun as well as an adventure, for there was always a promise that there might be something special on the other end of the line. Maybe even the "big one," that two-pound brook trout that didn't get away.

On May 30, 1979, less than two months after the fire, John Coffey came home from work looking forward to spending the holiday weekend with his family. He arrived with new fishing poles for his four children, Sean 10, Suzanne 9, Daniel 7, and Clancy 5. The kids were delighted with the gifts and eager to try them out. It was raining that afternoon but as soon as the rain let up, John gave Sean and his sister Suzanne some money to run to the bait and tackle shop nearby on Main Street, for worms, hooks, and bobbers.

When they arrived at the shop, they soon discovered that they were fifteen cents short of what they needed to complete their purchase. Undeterred, they quickly ran back home for the difference. They were happy to see that the rain was still holding off and that there would still be time to get back to the shop, complete the purchase, and return home in time to try out their new poles. For the Coffey kids, living near the water was by far the most exciting aspect of being temporarily relocated. The waterfall, the rowboats, and the fishermen, who wandered down the railroad tracks that ran aside the pond looking for the perfect spot to cast their lines, simply fascinated them.

When Sean and Suzanne arrived back home, their dad gave them the additional change needed and they quickly ran back to the main road, anxiously awaiting a break in the traffic so they could cross and complete their errand. Although she had already crossed busy Main Street twice, Suzanne felt suddenly afraid as they made their way across the street for their third time, and grabbed her brother's hand. Letting go when they reached the other side, they quickly made their way back into the shop, once a former garage connected to a large old clapboard home surrounded by a picket fence. Sean handed the balance to the cashier, grabbed the foam cup of earthworms while his sister took the bag, then both darted out of the shop headed for home. Sean was excited and wanted to get fishing as soon as possible. Suzanne quickly fell behind and yelled to her brother to slow down and wait for her. This was not uncommon, as Sean was usually a couple of steps ahead of his younger siblings.

By the time Suzanne reached the road, Sean had been struck head-on by a motor vehicle on the far side of the street. There are no words to describe the horror of that moment. One that has been relived countless times in Suzanne's mind over the years, often brought on totally unexpected by everyday triggers. Onlookers came to the scene and tried to help. A man yelled, "He's still breathing, call an ambulance." Suzanne turned around to see a young girl running to the edge of her fenced-in yard for a closer look. She screamed to the girl to call 9-1-1 and get help; then at the instruction of the same man, ran home to get her dad. Roy Shepherd, who owned and operated a lawn mower shop at this same location, and some others nearby, ran out into the street to see if they could help. Roy, a volunteer firefighter for many years, had recently become certified as an Emergency Medical Technician.

I was on patrol and received a radio transmission requesting I respond to a report of a child struck by a car in the vicinity of South and Main Streets. I was about three miles west of that location, activated my siren and blue warning lights, and immediately headed in that direction. As a precaution I requested that an ambulance be sent to this location and was advised one had already been dispatched. That was my first indication that I was heading into a bad situation. As I approached the intersection I saw a boy wearing jeans and a jean jacket lying in the roadway. I also noticed Roy Shepherd and knew I had someone with emergency medical expertise to work with. I stopped my police cruiser directly in front of the victim to provide protection from further injury for all of us. I grabbed my medical jump kit and ran to the child. He was unconscious, had no pulse, showed no sign of respiration, appeared cyanotic, and his pupils were fixed. He was also badly bruised with some minor bleeding which appeared to have stopped. My primary focus turned to his airway as I had concern that his neck might be fractured. The overall impact damage to his body was very visible which led me to believe an upper spinal fracture might exist. Working with Roy, we kept his neck straight and hyper-extended his chin in an attempt to maintain an open airway. He made no attempt to breathe on his own. He was clinically dead. Together we started to administer cardiopulmonary resuscitation and after a few breaths saw his skin color basically remain in a cyanotic state. Not a good sign. Not what I wanted.

Certainly not an answer to the demand, "Breathe, damn it, breathe!" that was running through my head. As I was working on the boy I felt a tap on my shoulder. I turned my head and looked at John Coffey, who told me he was the boy's father and asked, "Is he going to make it?" I responded, "I'm not sure," and continued to administer emergency care. Off in the distance I could hear the wail of a siren. I knew the ambulance crew was just moments away. They couldn't get there soon enough. The victim, Sean Coffey, age 10, John and Nancy Coffey's oldest child, was rushed to Nashoba Community Hospital and pronounced dead shortly after his arrival. After the ambulance departed I drove John to the hospital. We were met there shortly after by Nancy, who had been driven there by her boss. Not long after, I accompanied John into an enclosed room where he made a positive identification of his deceased child. A day that had started out on a happy note for the Coffey family had ended in tragedy.

Investigation showed Sean started to cross the street as the car that hit him approached. The operator of the vehicle that struck him was an elderly woman who stated that when she saw Sean she tried to stop but it was too late. Sean Coffey was buried at the Hillside Cemetery in Townsend. On his tombstone the following is inscribed; "ADVENTUROUS, LIGHT-HEARTED, CAREFREE – HE WANDERED NEAR AND FAR ... NOWHERE WILL HE BE MORE FREE."

# AFTERMATH:

I went out to lunch with John Coffey recently. He has two regrets about that day so long ago. The first, that the Commonwealth of Massachusetts hadn't done more to screen older drivers. He feels that maybe the driver's inability to react quicker contributed to his son being struck. Based on the law at the time the driver met all the requirements to operate a motor vehicle and was properly licensed. Although elderly, she was not speeding, and in the absence of any probable cause to believe otherwise, no criminal charges were filed against her. Massachusetts has made changes to better screen older drivers, but the age factor, as well as the degree of testing, still remains under debate. John's second regret was allowing Sean and Suzanne to run the errand to the bait and tackle shop. A normal regret based upon the very abnormal event that occurred, but a decision that any father perhaps would have made under the circumstances. John told me the one thing that kept him going, the one thing that got him through the loss of his oldest child were his other three children. He had to be strong for them. John Coffey still thinks of Sean everyday. His children still keep him going. The house that burned was rebuilt and he still works the family farm.

Nancy Coffey was at work when she was notified that a car had struck her son. Not knowing the details, her mind set was that he had perhaps suffered a broken arm or leg and would possibly have to undergo surgery. Her boss insisted on driving her to the hospital and when she asked him how badly her son had been hurt, he answered that he didn't know. She could not detect any indication in his facial expression to contradict his words. Not until she walked into the hospital and was told that her son died as a result of the injuries he suffered did it hit her. Being notified that her son had been killed didn't seem real. She was numbed by the news; shocked beyond belief.

The Coffeys left the hospital and were transported to a neighbor's home where their other three children had been taken. Nancy recalls not being able to move to get out of the car. She felt paralyzed. Surely she would awaken from her nightmare at any moment. She remembers a woman looking straight into her eyes and saying, "This may be the hardest thing you'll ever have to do, but you have to get out of the car." Not until then was she able to move. A moment in time she will never forget.

In 1991, twelve years after the accident, Nancy sought

professional counseling to deal with painful memories from 1979 and the aftermath. Over the years she had faced a variety of "happenings" that would trigger painful memories. There were the expected ones: holidays, birthdays, and the anniversary date of Sean's passing, but there was another that came unexpected when someone would ask, "How many children do you have?" The question triggered the memory of her loss and the dilemma of whether or not to "go there" with the person who had asked the question. She said in the beginning that particular question was difficult to deal with, since she often became tearful. She didn't want the other person to feel bad for having caused the tears, or perhaps even to regret having spoken to her at all. Eventually, as more time passed, it became easier as she learned to simply say, "I had four children, three surviving." Then the ball would be in the other person's court as to how they chose to respond.

Nancy recently told me she wished that they all had gone to counseling right after Sean's death, but back then there was a sort of stigma associated with going to counseling. So many people that could have benefited from it didn't go. What kept her going after the loss of her first-born child was her need to be strong for her three surviving children. Her love for her children, grandchildren, her faith in God, and her belief in Eternal Life gives her the power to move forward in a joyful way. Sean is always with her in her heart, and she firmly believes they will be reunited one day. Nancy is currently self-employed as a Licensed Massage Therapist helping to make a positive difference in other people's lives.

The marriage between John and Nancy broke up shortly after Sean's death. Something I saw many times during my law enforcement career after the death of a child. Suzanne was 9 years old when she saw her brother killed. After that day, the sound of an ambulance siren's wail brought tears to her eyes. She knew without a doubt that bad things can and do happen to people, especially those she knows and loves. For Suzanne, the fragrance of cut flowers became the smell of death, reminding her of the funeral. That terrible day she saw her dad cry, his shoulders, and his whole body shaking. She was also struck by the sound of her uncle crying loudly behind her. Men didn't cry, not until that day.

She found it difficult to speak of the tragedy for the first ten years after it happened without getting too upset to continue. She, her brother Daniel and sister Clancy struggled each in their own way with the loss of their brother and the many other losses that followed in the aftermath: the breakup of their family, the changed relationships, and watching their parents struggle trying to bring life back to "normal" for themselves and their children.

Suzanne coped with many of her struggles by focusing on school, her grades, and setting her sights on college and foreign travel. She graduated from high school in 1988 and moved to Washington, D.C. to study at American University where she earned her BA in International Studies and Russian Area Studies. She went on to complete her MBA from George Washington University, traveled internationally, and worked in the field of her study. She stayed in the Washington, D.C. area, married Oscar Camacho, and became the mother of two boys.

When she became a mom she grieved the loss of her brother a second time but this time from the perspective of a parent. She admits she may have been overprotective with her first child, avoids tragic news stories about children, and worries probably more than most about children near roads and in parking lots. Her loss has become a part of the woman she is, who carries a scar that is always there but less painful with the passing of time.

Our system of government has many faults. The amount of time and money it takes to accomplish simple projects in and for the Commonwealth of Massachusetts is astonishing. Privately owned businesses would fail if managed in similar fashion. Between politics and funding antics, years can be spent trying to accomplish simple tasks. There is now a traffic signal with a pedestrian crossing button at the intersection where Sean Coffey was killed. Rest assured, even in the face of such tragic loss, that signal took years to put in place and did not come easy.

On a sunlit wall inside the library of the Hawthorne Brook Middle School in Townsend there is a full-body framed painting of ten-year old Sean Coffey. He is standing near the water's edge with his fishing pole putting bait on his hook. Below the painting there is a plaque that reads, "IN MEMORY OF SEAN COFFEY – CLASS OF 83." The painting, a work by local artist Robert Johnson, was hung there over thirty years ago as a memorial to Sean by school staff that loved him as one of their own. That's what teachers do best, although they are often viewed solely as educators. With the exiting of personnel and the passing of time, people have forgotten who the boy in the painting is, and why his image adorns the wall. Erasing the past is a task that time excels at, or so we think. The hands upon life's clock cannot be turned back, but every now and then conditions exist that require they be adjusted.

# CHAPTER 6

## SAD SITUATION
### FALL 1979

I was a sergeant working a four to midnight shift one cold November evening in 1979. My radio communications center dispatched me to the power station just off Main Street east of the center of town to investigate a report of a scantily clad woman seen in that area. The power station, located on a short dead-end paved driveway, was simply a series of large electrical transformers enclosed within a high chain link fence with barbwire surrounding the top. With the exception of one dull streetlight, the area was for the most part quite dark and desolate. As I pulled my police cruiser into the paved entrance, my headlights illuminated a young woman wearing only a bra and panties. I activated my blue lights and stopped just in front of where she was standing. She appeared to be in shock, her body shivering, her arms folded across her chest. I exited my cruiser, told her I was a police officer, and approached her. She was crying and became so hysterical I couldn't understand what she was trying to tell me. She was dirty. Clearly she had been on the ground at some point. Her underwear had both grass and dirt stains, and her hair was messed and filthy. She also had an odor of alcohol coming from her mouth. I took her by the arm and walked her back to the passenger side of my cruiser, opened the door, and had her sit down. I then retrieved a blanket from the trunk of my car for her to wrap herself up in. I didn't know exactly what had happened to this young woman but I had every reason to believe she had been raped. At my request an ambulance came and took her to Burbank Hospital, about eleven miles west of my location. I followed the ambulance to the hospital.

I waited in the emergency room for about an hour before the doctor attending her met with me. He advised that the young woman had not been sexually assaulted, but had been pushed out of a parked vehicle after an argument with her boyfriend. Aside from psychological abuse, she only suffered from minor scrapes and bruises. The doctor further advised that her parents had been notified of her condition and were on their way to the hospital from upstate New York to pick up their daughter. He then asked me to stay at the hospital until the girl's parents arrived, as there was some concern based upon his patient's agitated mental state that she might attempt to flee the hospital on her own. Although I had the authority to apprehend her if she did, I agreed to stay with her in a private room rather than risk putting her and myself, or some other officer, in a position of possible physical confrontation during her arrest. All of which could end up with possible injury and a court proceeding that would leave her with a permanent arrest record.

I entered a private room at the hospital and introduced myself to the young woman I first met at the power station. Although she had been cleaned up she still appeared untidy in our sanitized setting. She was wearing two blue and white hospital johnnies, the first facing forward, the other reversed. At first she had nothing to say to me. Not even "Hello." Sensing tension in the room I just sat across from her not saying anything either. After a few minutes she asked, "Ya got any cigarettes?" This was a welcomed question because it opened the door for me. She gave me a place to start. "No, I don't smoke," was my reply. "Do you have a name?" I asked in return. "Why do you want to know?" she asked with scorn in her voice. "Well," I said, "I have money on me, there's a cigarette machine down the hall, and I might be able to get permission to take you outside so you can have a smoke. In order to do that however it would be nice to be able to tell the nurse your name and that we are friends." Talk about a change in attitude. "My name is Megan," she responded. I had played this one-on-one game so many times with young people I knew what the next move would be while they tried to figure out what the next move should be. My next move, "Do you have a last name?" Megan's move, "Kankowski." Thus the game began. Very seldom did people state their last names. Even in this situation. She wasn't in trouble with me but I was certain her parents wouldn't be pleased with her once they arrived. Nonetheless, we played the game. She didn't know it but she was up against the master.

My first order of business was to let Megan have a cigarette. I told her that I was going to loan her five dollars, not give it to her. I made it clear that I expected her to repay the debt. I wanted her to feel obligated to me and take ownership of that obligation. I let her know that at some point down the road I expected my money back, although I figured I would never see it again. I also told her that smoking was not good for her health and if she wanted cigarettes she would have to put the money in the machine, not me. With that we walked down the hall where I watched as Megan bought a pack of cigarettes that came with a book of matches. From there we walked outside via the non-public entrance to the emergency room where Megan lit up. Amazing how easy it was to win the game. A few kind words and a cigarette – game over. I had won; again.

After her smoke, we walked back to the private room and continued talking. She wasn't a rebellious teen anymore and I wasn't the figure of authority I had been moments before. Megan told me how she had been with her boyfriend and how they rode in his car from her home in New York. She told me she had been drinking and didn't realize she was so far from home. She went on to say she had consensually "made out" with her boyfriend in the parking area where I found her, but refused his final advances. With that he shoved her out of the car and left. Megan was not unlike most other young people I knew. She had plans for the future and had a goal of becoming a hairdresser. She had a very real concern of how angry her parents would be with her once they arrived. I told her as bad as she might think her situation was she had to be honest with her parents. I assured her that parents have a way of understanding, especially if they are told the truth. She listened. She was by every indication, except for her smoking habit, a healthy normal teenager. We continued to talk, and she continued to smoke for the next four hours until her parents arrived to pick her up.

I met Megan's parents before she did in another private room. They were very nice and appreciative, but not pleased with their daughter's actions. I explained the circumstances surrounding Megan being transported to the hospital. I suggested that what their daughter needed at this moment in her life was love and understanding. I recommended on their long ride home that they let Megan open up to them rather than fire questions at her. I let them know that as bad as the evening seemed to be Megan had made good decisions as well, and what she needed most was a hug from someone who really loved her. With that the three of us walked to the room where Megan was waiting for us. Not much was said as they hugged one another and the tears began to flow. I gave each of them my business card, wished them well, and left them to be alone together.

## AFTERMATH:

Two years went by and Megan became a distant memory. I would think of her every now and then when driving past the power station entrance. A vanishing thought of sorts that drifted away as quickly as it arrived, replaced by one of more urgent importance. In July of 1981 an envelope arrived in the mail with my name hand written on the outside, marked "PERSONAL." I opened the envelope, unfolded the enclosed letter, and a five-dollar bill fell out onto my desk. The letter was from Megan. She thanked me for finding her on what she wrote was the "worst night of my life." She went on to write, "I have put my life back together and still live at home with my parents. I graduated from cosmetology school a month ago and I'm working at a beauty shop near my home. Enclosed is the five dollars I owe you. Love,

Megan." At the bottom she included a postscript, "P.S. Just so you know, I quit smoking."

# CHAPTER 7

# THE WEST ELM STREET TRIANGLE
## 1977 to 1981

There were three people directly connected to one another who lived on West Elm Street in West Townsend. Two of them didn't know they were attached in triplicate fashion even though the very existence of the first and third depended upon the generosity of the second. Over time this ongoing interaction of people became known to me as the "West Elm Street Triangle." Unlike the "Bermuda Triangle" off the Florida coast, there wasn't any great mystery to be unraveled. In fact the second person, the one who bestowed great kindness on the first, didn't even know there was a third person. Didn't know a triangular relationship was going on. Nor did the third. The first person, however, was quite aware of the triangle. He was the missing link the other two didn't know about. Without him the triangle wouldn't have existed.

This first person was Marshall, age 71, who lived on the upper end of West Elm Street in a small mobile home that blended into the landscape. Marshall's home provided the basic needs for someone existing solely on social security. Marshall didn't live alone, however. He lived with the one he loved. The one he knew he could always turn to when times got bad. Marshall was having a love affair with the wine bottle. Been going on for years. The whole town knew about it. The two of them could often be seen together sitting out in front of Marshall's bungalow snuggled together, the bottle gently caressed against his chest. They often slept together there as well, Marshall's head slumped down, and the bottle slumped next to him, his mind fogged over in the cast of a setting summer sun. A sight of intoxicated peace to those few that noticed. No one had to wonder what went on behind closed doors at Marshall's place because the same thing went on outside as well. I would stop while on evening patrol now and then and help Marshall to bed when he and his lover overdid it. When the evening chill dictated that Marshall should be on the other side of his door in a warm bed. I would make sure he got to where he should be after the bottle got the best of him. Made sure his lover was right there in plain view too so when he woke up he knew he wasn't alone. Some would say this was the wrong thing to do. Helping him stagger to bed was proper, but allowing his lover to spend the night was for some, inappropriate. Disgraceful. Who was I to make that decision? The man was in love. Attracted to the only lady that brought some sense of solace into his world. My duty was to keep Marshall safe as best I could, not suggest there was a better way of life. For Marshall there wasn't, and even if I said there was he wouldn't have listened anyway. Men in love are deaf to the words of wisdom and only hear the whisper of their lover; "Hold me close and let me warm you all over until we fall asleep together in each other's arms." That's what the bottle's soft voice always murmured into Marshall's ear. Most people heard the ocean when they put a wine bottle to their ear. Not Marshall. He just heard the "warm all over" and the "fall asleep together" stuff, followed by "I love you." That's what Marshall heard. That's what gave him comfort. Of course Marshall didn't put the bottle to his ear, he put it to his mouth, the nucleus of their relationship. When the lip of the bottle came into contact with his. For Marshall this was an act of love, not a quenching of his thirst. He often made this passionate kiss, over and over, day after day, into the evening hours until falling into a romantic stupor. He became so intoxicated at times he'd forget her name, but she never his. Her warmth ran deep through Marshall's veins right into his very soul. She would readily satisfy. She would aptly appease. She would always deliver. There wasn't any rolling of the waves to be heard in Marshall's bottle, just the sound of the woman he loved. Her name was Red Rose. Some would say she was attractive with her slender neck and robust body, but she wasn't low maintenance. Not by any means. Most would consider her a whore, because there was always an upfront price to pay before the act of love began. This "pay before play" was the only real problem Marshall ever had with her.

About a half-mile down the street from Marshall's place was the second person in the triangle. Her name was Marion, and like Marshall, she didn't live alone either. She shared her single story home with the one she loved too, the Holy Bible. Slept right beside her on the night table next to her bed. They would spend the last waking moments of each day together before Marion would fall off to sleep. On occasion they slept together, but that was seldom. Marion's bed was for sleeping only and served no other purpose, except when she was confined to it for a severe case of the flu. Marion had never married in the conventional sense. Most doubted she ever had a man in her life. Instead she had a life-long relationship with God and the Baptist Church, which was just about a half-mile from her home on Main Street. Had been involved in this relationship ever since she was a young girl in grammar school. Unlike Marshall, who needed daily doses of Red Rose to keep him going, Marion only required one act of love a week to keep her satisfied. Her every need was fulfilled each Sunday morning. Right there in the second pew, third seat in on the left, her very own ringside seat to view God in all his greatness. A place where she could feel his warmth and goodness up close and personal. He was her man, and the only man, central to her existence. He bestowed upon her a special kind of affection on Sunday that would last the entire week. A warming of her body and mind that lasted until the following Saturday leaving her with a craving for more. For certain, a feeling no other man could ever give her. An occasional bean supper or Bible study meeting in the basement of the church just added fuel to her fiery relationship with God. In her early sixties, Marion was in love with a much older man and she didn't care what people had to say about it either. She was after all, like Marshall, in love.

Marion was a good Christian who learned early on to "love thy neighbor." She cared about her community and for those less fortunate. The downtrodden. One of these poor souls was Marshall. Marion could plainly see that Marshall was possessed by the devil. Knew that the evil spirit that took hold of Marshall's life lived in a bottle. The same one that Red Rose lived in, but Marion only saw an evil spirit inside. Never the lady Marshall saw. Always felt Marshall was having an affair with a demon, not a lover. In Marshall, Marion also saw the skeleton of an alcoholic, and knew beneath the fragile form of wrinkled skin and shrunken bone of a once larger man, existed a human soul. One that God loved. Marion saw not the desperation of an alcoholic, but the soul of a sinner in need of saving. Worth saving, for God loved all of mankind. She refused to recognize a man who would rather drink than eat, but saw a lost soul that needed to eat rather than drink. For her the preservation of Marshall's body was the key to saving his soul. She knew if Marshall was allowed to continue along the path he had chosen, the possibility of death from malnutrition was just as real as cirrhosis of the liver, perhaps even greater. She was in a three-way race that pitted her against starvation and sin, but was determined to be the winner. She knew in order to save Marshall's soul she had to save his body first, the easier of the two to fix. She knew that proper nutrition could quickly bring Marshall's body back, but also knew that saving his soul would take time. Ridding his soul of the devil would require every ounce of strength she could muster. She could feel God's presence standing in her corner. He had been there for her for many years. Talking to her. Encouraging her. She was ready for the fight she was determined to win. One she knew she couldn't lose. She had God on her side.

Marion would do her grocery shopping on Friday and even though she lived alone, with the exception of the Bible, she shopped for two people. Everything she needed for herself was placed into bags destined for her home, while the basic essentials for a man living a solitary sinful existence were put into a separate bag for Marshall. I would occasionally see Marion bring a bag of groceries to Marshall's home. She never entered to the best of my knowledge. Just parked her old Chevy in the driveway and stood at his doorstep, her arms extended in open generosity with the bag in hand. Marshall leaning up against the door jam just inside, seeming tired from overdoing it one more time with Red Rose. Marion would do this once a week. Trying as best she could to get Marshall's body in shape so his soul could be shaped up and saved, too. A double act of kindness really, all in one bag.

Harland, the third face of the triangle, lived on West Elm Street, too. Right up the street from Marion and just down the street from Marshall. In the middle, give or take a couple hundred feet. Harland lived alone as well, and found comfort working in his vegetable garden. Supplied him with something constructive to do, as well as nourishment for his body. During the winter months he really didn't do much other than try to keep warm. Read a book now and then, but not the Bible. Put his lip to the bottle too, mostly to get a sip of ginger ale or taste of milk. Wasn't in love with anyone or anything really, except his garden, but that was a seasonal affair. He, like Marion and Marshall, counted on his monthly Social Security check to survive. Harland was the third leg of the West Elm Street Triangle but he didn't know it. Marion didn't know it either. In fact neither knew the West Elm Street Triangle even existed, but Marshall did. Marshall was that all-important missing link. The catalyst that kept three people connected even though two of them didn't know they were joined. In his own way he was a master of deception.

Every Friday Marion would leave Marshall standing just inside his front door, grocery bag in hand, enough food to keep him going for the week ahead. Marion would drive away knowing she had done the right thing. Deep down inside she knew this Christian act of love for her neighbor would be rewarded. For in time she knew Marshall would see the light. With a strong body he could tell Red Rose it was over. Kick her out the door and out of his life. In fact Marion could visualize Marshall going to Sunday service. She knew Marshall's conversion would take time. Something she had plenty of. She knew her persistence and patience would pay off in the long run.

Marshall on the other hand was in it for the moment, the short haul. He said all the right things to Marion when she dropped off the groceries. Let her know he appreciated her. Told her he was trying as best he could, but for him life was a struggle, especially with what he called "his problem." If only Marion had parked just down the street instead of going straight home she would have become aware of the West Elm Street Triangle. She would have seen the light, but not in a Christian way. She would have caught on to Marshall and realized saving his soul was a far greater task than she ever imagined. She never did though. She just went quickly on her way, feeling good about doing the right thing.

Marshall would wait until he saw Marion's old Chevy disappear out of sight down West Elm Street. With his left arm still around the bag of groceries he'd stick his head inside the door to give Red Rose a quick kiss goodbye, and then head off toward Harland's house. Harland was expecting him. Same thing happened every Friday. Could almost set your watch by it. Marshall didn't knock on Harland's door, just walked right in. After a few words of small talk Marshall would sell Harland everything in the bag for fifty-cents on the dollar. Marshall would pocket the money without counting it, not that he trusted Harland as much as he trusted himself. He knew within fifteen minutes he'd be taking the money back out of his pocket anyway. Once he got to the package store on Main Street. There he'd turn the cash into the love of his life. Red Rose would go home with him and the West Elm Street Triangle would disappear for another week leaving Marion's heart feeling blessed, Harland's stomach feeling full, and Marshall's soul feeling happy. Not saved, just happy. That's what Red Rose did for Marshall. Made him happy.

# AFTERMATH:

Marshall passed away in 1981. He didn't die alone. Red Rose was with him when he passed. He appeared very much in death like he did in life, alone with Red Rose, who sat expressionless as she always had. She didn't care though; she wouldn't be alone for long. She knew there'd be another daddy waiting for her just down the road. Harland came to grips with the loss of Marshall and started to pay full price for his groceries once again. Marion, who appeared unknowing all along, knew more than what appeared on the surface. I had assumed she was trying to save Marshall's soul but who was I to judge? What she did do was very obvious. She provided Marshall with the knowledge that someone truly cared about him. Every week he knew there was a kind soul who'd stop by and check on him. If he ever doubted there was God in heaven he knew there was Marion on earth. Obviously Marion was Christian to the core and openly practiced God's many teachings. For her, "love thy neighbor" was more than just words written in scripture. Did she save Marshall's soul? I'll never know, but I can tell you one thing, she certainly touched mine.

# CHAPTER 8

## WEST SIDE STORY
### SUMMER 1979

In light of the last segment, "The West Elm Street Triangle," the following true story is worth telling even though I wasn't directly involved at the outset. Bob Tumber owned and operated the West Side Package Store throughout my entire police career. The store, located on Main Street in West Townsend, was the size of a small cape-style home. In the center of the building there was a main entrance, which consisted of two steps with black metal handrails on each side. Bob was considered the unofficial mayor of West Townsend and carried an equal amount of political clout in Townsend Center as well. The store was white in color, and because Bob was so well connected around town, his place was called the "White House." Many discussions about town affairs and politics were held there. At the Town Hall, in the center of town where town business was governed, there were public forums in which "old business," "new business," and "none of your business" were discussed. The latter, "none of your business," were actually "executive sessions" that were held behind closed doors. Hidden from the public. There were no "executive sessions" at the West Side Package Store. There were no closed doors to hide behind. Everything was everybody's business. National, state, or local government actions were open season at Bob's. I tried to stop by Bob's store at least three times a week. He kept me up to speed about things I needed to know as the chief law enforcement officer of the community, as well as the latest joke going around town.

I sometimes ate my lunch at Bob's, which usually consisted of three pretzel sticks and a small bottle of cranberry juice. Bob sold liquor, beer, and wine, but he also sold various staples such as milk and bread. Bob would allow people to charge their milk, bread, and whatever else they needed for the dinner table. I know some of the debt he incurred with his milk and bread credit system was never recouped. He once told me, "Hey, if they can't afford to pay for it, they need the milk and bread more than I do." Bob was good to people, even if a few of his debtors weren't good to him.

Marshall, the main man in the West Elm Street Triangle was also central to another ongoing saga, in this case, the "West Side Story." He shared a close friendship with two other guys about his age. The first was Randy, retired and living alone, lived just up the street from Marshall on West Elm Street. The other guy was Muskrat, who lived alone as well, just over the state line in southern New Hampshire. Marshall was the man in charge. He was in every respect, the "leader of the pack." Randy was the owner of an old Ford pickup truck. The kind that was easy to fix with a pair of pliers and a screwdriver, not like the computerized models of today. Sure it had a few dents on the outside but it got everyone from point "A," West Elm Street, to point "B," the West Side Package Store, and then safely back to point "A" again. Muskrat on the other hand didn't own anything. As his nickname implied, he was just a small rodent dressed in human attire. He was always on the move, sniffing around, looking for the free handout. The common bond between these three men was Red Rose, the gal who lived in the bottle. They all loved her dearly. They shared her openly. The only time these three guys fought was when Red Rose wasn't around. They didn't fight over her; they fought in absence of her.

On a warm Friday afternoon just after Marion had left her weekly bag of groceries at Marshall's house, Randy stopped by with Muskrat to visit. They sat around and kissed Red Rose one at a time on the same spot, just above her neck. Everyone was happy until Red Rose disappeared. Then all hell broke loose and Muskrat got beat up. That was how it always happened. Muskrat was a small man weighing slightly over 140 pounds. Marshall and Randy on the other hand were heavyweights, evenly matched. Neither was able to inflict much damage on the other. Regretfully, rather than pound on their own chests to show their dominance, they pounded on Muskrat's instead. Based on the black eyes Muskrat displayed over the years I would suggest they pounded on his head too. Muskrat never filed a complaint against either of them so I just watched from a distance. These three men were modern day "Three Musketeers." When Red Rose was around it was "all for one, one for all." When she wasn't, it was "every man for himself." Muskrat of course was always the loser.

On this particular Friday, after the main event was over and things quieted down, Marshall suggested that the three of them take his freshly delivered groceries down to Harland's house, cash them in, and then go pick up Red Rose down at Bob's place. Randy looked at Marshall and said, "Marshall you possess the most perspicacious mind of any man I have ever encountered. You are a sagacious soul sailing upon a vast ocean of wisdom. Your perception and astuteness runs deep like the waters you sail upon. You are a man that adheres to ethical principles and personal dignity. I look upon you with great esteem and feel privileged to have the honor of driving you to Bob's." Randy had an extensive vocabulary, what Muskrat called "a way with words," but Randy also knew where his bread was buttered. In this case the bread was in Marshall's grocery bag and needed to be converted into cash, not buttered. Their meeting with Red Rose depended on Randy's driving skills to get Marshall to Harland's house and then on to Bob's store. As far as Randy was concerned, the sooner they got there, the better.

Bob was alone in his store standing behind the main counter facing the front door. He had an excellent view of the main entrance and all that was going on outside. He was lost in his thoughts when he heard a loud banging noise. In disbelief he watched as Randy's pickup crashed through the left handrail, bounced across the front steps, through the right handrail, coming to rest in a bush on the right front side of the store. Bob ran out to see if anyone was hurt and was pleased to find no one was injured. Bob could easily see that Randy had driven about six inches too close to the main entrance when he drove into the parking lot. Randy got out of the pickup appearing as nothing had happened and said hello to Bob. Bob, not amused with the amount of damage done to his property, asked Randy what had happened. Randy seemed confused by Bob's question. As far as he was concerned nothing had happened. So Bob said, "Randy you just drove in and hit my front steps and handrails." Randy looked at Bob and said, "Really? I did that? Are you sure Bob?" Of course Bob was sure and he was also certain that Red Rose had influenced Randy's poor judgment. By this time both Marshall and Muskrat had gotten out of the truck, looking a bit confused as well. They too were under the influence of Red Rose. Randy then said, "Well if I did do that damage Bob I'm very sorry, you have my most humble and deepest apology." Bob had a second problem on his hand. He had to get these three safely back to West Elm Street. Bob reached into Randy's pickup and took out the ignition key. He then turned toward the "Three Musketeers" and said, "Look I'm going to drive all of you home in my car. Give me a couple of minutes to lock up the store. Understand?" They must have because no one answered Bob's question.

Within a few minutes all four of them were in Bob's 1963 Ford Falcon headed toward West Elm Street. Bob was driving, Randy was in the front passenger seat, Marshall sat right behind Randy, and Muskrat behind Bob. As they drove along Randy started to talk. "You know, Bob, everyone calls me Randy but my real name is Randolph. I've been inflexible all my life, I've worked diligently for years, but I'm just a detriment to society. Let me extrapolate." Muskrat, hearing what Randy had just said, asked to no one in particular, "What's extrapyalate mean?" Randy, speaking directly to Muskrat, said, "The word isn't pronounced 'ex-trap-ya-late', it's pronounced 'ex-trap-o-late', and it means to use known facts as a starting point from which to draw inferences or conclusions about something unknown." "Really?" exclaimed Muskrat, "Where do you come up with that kind of stuff?" Randy, sensing the ignorance of the question, ignored it, and began talking to Bob again. "You know, Bob, you possess the most perspicacious mind of any man I have ever encountered. You are a sagacious soul sailing upon a vast ocean of wisdom. Your perception and astuteness runs deep like the waters you sail upon. You are a man that adheres to ethical principles and personal dignity. I look upon you with great esteem and feel privileged to have you driving me home this afternoon." Marshall, sitting in the back, having heard something quite similar moments before, just sat quietly and listened. "You know, Bob," Randy continued, "I've been deeply disturbed lately. I've looked back over my life and what have I accomplished? Zilch! Not a single solitary thing. Not even a small segment of something sizable. I'm no good to anyone. When I get home I'm going to take my shotgun out and blow my brains out." Marshall, hearing Randy verbalize his intent of self destruction, tapped Bob on the shoulder and said, "Bob if you don't mind, do you think you could swing back by the store so I can get a quart of Red Rose before Randy blows his brains out?"

# AFTERMATH:

Everyone arrived home safely and Bob got his front entrance fixed. One night about three months later I responded to yet another call for a fight at Randy's house. While responding to the call along West Elm Street I spotted Muskrat walking toward his New Hampshire home. I stopped and noticed he was sporting a "new" black eye. He told me he had just been in a fight with Randy. I didn't have to ask him what the fight was over. I already knew. Red Rose. I continued on to Randy's home and parked my cruiser just down from his driveway. In the police business you never show up at the front door on a disturbance call.

I walked down the long dark driveway toward the house and swung open an iron gate about two hundred feet from Randy's front door. The gate made a screeching sound, as it swung slowly open. This was followed by an unexpected shotgun blast. Shotguns have a distinctive sound that really gets your attention, especially when its pitch black, you can't see the shooter, and you think it was just fired at you. I drew my service weapon and yelled, "Randy, it's me, Sergeant May, put the gun down. I want to talk with you." With that the front door swung open and I could clearly see Randy silhouetted, standing without the weapon. He yelled back, "Okay Billy, I didn't know it was you. I thought you were Muskrat coming back. That son of a bitch!" I figured Randy was pretty upset. He called Muskrat a "son of a bitch" instead of "a man of despicable character lacking integrity." I could tell by the tone of his voice, as well as the vocabulary he was using, he was quite disturbed. "I'm really sorry about that Billy. A man of your distinguished character does truly not deserve to be treated in such hostile fashion. I extend to you my deepest apology. Please come on in."

I went inside and saw the shotgun standing in the corner. I also noticed an empty bottle of Red Rose on the kitchen counter. I went over, picked the shotgun up, cracked the breach open, and found the gun was empty. Even so, I sat at the kitchen table with me between Randy and the shotgun. Randy continued to tell me about the fight he had with Muskrat and how he had simply fired a "warning shot" into the air to let the "rat" know he meant business. I listened, knowing part of my success hinged upon being a good listener, but in this case I really didn't have to. I had heard the story so many times before I knew it by heart. I left Randy's house with his firearms license in my pocket and his empty shotgun in my hand. Muskrat was gone. His shotgun was gone, and the love of his life, Red Rose, was gone too. Randy wasn't worried though, he knew Red Rose would be back.

# CHAPTER 9

# KATIE DUNBAR
## SUMMER 1986

In the summer of 1986 I was living in a ranch-style home on a quiet street in Townsend. The traffic along this street consisted mostly of families that lived there so vehicle speed was not an issue. So much so that some parents would allow their children to ride their bikes up and down the street. I lived halfway down the street and would park my unmarked police cruiser near the roadway to slow any fast moving vehicles down. Unmarked police cruisers stand out just as much as the marked ones do. All the kids in the neighborhood knew that I was a police officer and it was not uncommon for them to stop and say hello if they saw me outside.

One of these little people was Katie Dunbar, who lived four doors down and across the street from me with her parents and two siblings. Katie was a pretty, blonde four-year-old who had a smile that could melt your heart. I had taken the morning off because I had planned to work late in the evening. There was a garage attached to my home and I had decided to install two six-foot storage shelves on both sides on an interior chimney that ran up the wall. The morning was warm and I had the garage door open to allow for the natural sunlight to illuminate my work area. I was using wood to construct the shelving and was in the process of assembling my masterpiece when Katie rode her two-wheeler into the garage singing "Tomorrow," made famous by the musical "Annie." She just rode right in happily singing away as if the world was her audience. She just belted the song out. "Tomorrow, tomorrow, it's almost tomorrow, it's only AH ----- DAY, AH ----- WAY!" I don't know for sure but I think Katie was rehearsing in her mind for her lead role on Broadway. Her rendition of the song was priceless. One of those special moments in life you never forget. After completing the song she got off her bike, put the kickstand down and walked over to me and said, "Hi Chief, what are you doing?" I looked down at my little neighbor and said, "Well Katie, I'm making new storage shelves for my garage." "Why are you doing that?" she inquired. "To make extra places to put all my stuff," I replied. "Why do you need extra places for all your stuff?" she continued. I sensed our conversation was headed down the well-known question and answer road. A path only a child can take you down. The one that's strewn with little inquisitive verbal bumps that add so much pleasure to the trip. "Well to be honest with you Katie, I've got so much stuff I don't have enough places to put it all," I replied. She just stood there watching me, quite satisfied with my answer. I was anticipating her next question, which I felt, would evolve around how I had accumulated so much stuff but it never came. As she watched I raised a board in place, put a nail where I wanted it, and as I went to strike the nail with my hammer, hit my finger instead. The intense pain caused a whole variety of four letter words to immediately gather in my mind. In a split second they had assembled and marched immediately to the tip of my tongue waiting to rush out and help relieve the instant agony I had just suffered. My very own army of verbal vulgar volunteers, ready to help reduce my stress level that had gone from very low after hearing Katie sing, to off the chart once the hammer struck my finger. In that small microsecond of time I knew I needed a word I could shout out that would help me recover, but more importantly, could be said in the presence of a four-year-old. For some reason I yelled out, "PRUNES!" Why? I don't know, but that's what came out. Poor Katie's eyes grew to the size of silver dollars. She immediately put her hands to her ears in an apparent attempt to block out what she just heard. With a shocked expression on her face she yelled back, "Chief, what you just said!" With that she quickly kicked up her kick stand, jumped back on her bicycle, rode out of the garage, and headed for home as fast as her little feet could pedal. As bad as it seemed for Katie I felt good about maintaining my cool and controlling my mouth under such trying circumstances.

I was in my office the next day when I received a telephone call from Katie's mom Claire. She told me how Katie came running into the house out of breath to tell her that the Chief had used a four-letter word. She said she asked Katie what four-letter word and Katie replied, "Prunes." Claire went on to explain to Katie that the word prunes had six letters, and that is was alright to say prunes, further explaining to Katie what a prune actually was. Claire also went on to say the last time she hit her finger with a hammer she didn't have the presence of mind to say prunes and came out with something far worse.

# AFTERMATH:

My little friend Katie is now married and has two children of her own. I talked with Katie not long ago and asked her if she had ever hit her finger with a hammer. "Oh yes," she told me. Then I popped the big question, "Well, what did you yell Katie?" She was quiet for a moment and replied, "Prunes! What did you expect?" Whenever I hear the song "Tomorrow" I think of Katie, the little girl in my garage. Especially on cloudy days, because I know the sun will come out tomorrow. I have hit my finger a few times since 1986 when no one was around. "Prunes" never rose to the tip of my tongue on those occasions, however. Guess what did?

# CHAPTER 10

## RYAN LIELASUS
### SUMMER 1986

Hanging next to the portrait of Sean Coffey in the library at Hawthorne Brook Middle School there is another painting of similar size, created by the same artist, Robert Johnson. The second one is a rendition of Ryan Lielasus, who was a student at the school for just one day! For him not to be remembered at Hawthorne Brook is understandable; no one had the opportunity to get to know him. The painting shows Ryan, age 13, with wavy hair wearing his Little League uniform with a green and white-striped jacket covering his upper body. Straddling his red mountain bike with his left foot on the ground, his right on the opposite pedal, a right-handed baseball glove strapped to the handlebar, he appears to have just arrived at the ballpark. There is a pensive look in Ryan's eyes as he stares out from his portrait. This is Ryan's story.

I first met Ryan Lielasus one afternoon while he and a friend were riding their four-wheel all terrain vehicles in Townsend. The boys were riding along railroad tracks owned by the Boston and Maine Railroad. The railroad company had asked that we stop anyone from using their property in an attempt to avoid complications that can result from such use. Although trains no longer used the track there was concern by company officials that someone could get injured. As a boy I often jumped into the Squannacook River from a railroad trestle in the center of town and walked the tracks to get from one place to another. So when I stopped Ryan and his friend my primary concern wasn't about their trespassing on railroad property. I was, however, concerned with the boys use of their recreational vehicles on property, both public and private, without consent of the owners. Not so much specific minor motor vehicle laws in place that governed their use, but the civil ramifications that could result should someone get hurt. The boys were young, so instead of utilizing my "Option A" or "Option B" method of motor vehicle law enforcement normally applied to older teens, I simply had them park their vehicles and drove them home to talk with their parents about my concern and the problem.

Ryan grew up in Ashby, Massachusetts, on Old County Road with his mother and father, Carol and Richard Lielasus, and older bothers Mark and Craig. He attended Ashby Elementary School just up the street from his home and enjoyed playing baseball, basketball, soccer, and chess. He also participated in Cub Scouts and Boy Scouts, earning many merit badges while climbing up through the ranks. The towns of Ashby and Townsend border one another and are members of the North Middlesex Regional School District. Children living in Ashby attended Ashby Elementary School from first through sixth grade, and then transferred to Hawthorne Brook Middle School in Townsend for their seventh and eighth grade classes. After that they would go on to North Middlesex Regional High School, also located in Townsend. On Wednesday, September 3, 1986, Ryan started his first day of seventh grade at Hawthorne Brook Middle School. He enjoyed the excitement of starting in a new school with some new faces and was perhaps a little apprehensive with such a major change in his life. Even the school bus ride was different, taking much more time than earlier years. Later that day after supper, Ryan rode his bicycle to the weekly band concert in the center of town. This would be the final band concert of the year. The one that placed young and old alike on notice that summer was unofficially over. The last time people would gather in mass outside under the stars to enjoy the friendly warmth of the season.

Juha Valikangas grew up in Ashby as well, not far from Ryan. Although Juha was two years older than Ryan they were good friends and hung out together, usually playing basketball on the public court in the center of town, or baseball at the town field. So it was not unusual that the two of them would meet at the basketball court just before the band concert started. The boys were in transition, going from those early double digits of tranquil existence into those teenager years of wonder and excitement. For them, their change from one to the other was occurring in small town America, where alcohol and illicit drugs were not part of their existence. The talk that evening centered on many subjects, perhaps the most important of which was girls. So it wasn't the music that attracted them to the band concert when the music first started to play, as much as it was the sound of voices they would hear from the girls they knew would be there. Enticed by both, the latter perhaps creating the stronger pull, they set off to be with their friends. On a summer night in Ashby the band concert in the center of town was the place to be.

Midway through the concert there was an intermission and the band stopped playing. Ryan and Juha walked across the street to join a group that had gathered on the steps of the local library, not an uncommon occurrence on band concert night. There was a small group mingled there when Richard Alexander drove up in an older model green Dodge Omni. Richard had just received his license to operate a motor vehicle in Massachusetts and asked if anyone wanted to go for a ride. Clifford Lapore jumped into the front passenger seat, while Josh White-McFarland, Juha, and Ryan climbed into the back. Josh sat on the left, Juha in the middle, and Ryan on the right. Richard had set up two speakers in wooden fruit crates in the rear of the car, so the back seat area was confining. They left the library and headed out of town toward Piper Road, the music from the radio playing very loud in the back. The vehicle was traveling at a high rate of speed when they came upon a section of the roadway that changed from pavement to gravel. There was also a slight curve at this same location. It was at this point that Richard lost control of the vehicle, as it slid sideways, one way and then the other over the loose gravel surface. The out-of-control Dodge climbed an embankment and rolled over while the passengers heard the scraping of metal against metal and the smashing of glass. Then there was silence. The smell of hot engine oil blended in with that of spilled radiator and window washer fluid. Richard was ejected from the vehicle, coming to rest under the roof of the car. Juha was injured but managed to pull himself from the wreckage, as did Clifford and Josh. Ryan was unresponsive. The three boys that got out on their own worked to free Richard from under the car, who was taking shallow breaths. Although injured, Juha made his way some distance to Martha Perkin's home, the only house in the area, where he collapsed while she called for help.

# AFTERMATH:

Ryan died in the crash and was pronounced dead at the scene by the medical examiner. Police notified Carol of his death later that evening and her first reaction was "You have to be kidding!" She had watched Ryan leave their home earlier in the evening on his bicycle. How could Ryan go from riding his bike to being killed in an automobile accident? Not hit by a motor vehicle while riding his bike, but fatally injured as a passenger. It just didn't make any sense. She was overwhelmed by the tragic news. Ryan was her baby. Certainly what she had been told couldn't be true, but as her home started to fill with family and friends, the realization that she had lost her youngest child started to quickly set in. She clearly remembers sitting down that evening, her legs shaking uncontrollably. From that moment, events that followed became a blur. The funeral was overpowering with an outpouring of people. Ryan's father and older brothers would go on and deal with their loss in their own individual way. The Lielasus family would never be the same.

From the outset of the tragedy Carol told me she started to feel weird. Her best explanation being that people around her seemed the same as they always had but she felt different. She held back from conversation. She didn't know what to say, didn't know what would be said. If asked how many children she had, without hesitation she would respond, "I have three, I lost my youngest one." For the first year after losing Ryan she couldn't sleep and would leave the television on all night simply to make noise. She slept in her son's bed one night to feel closer to him. When sleep would take hold of her she would dream about him and one night dreamt she saw Ryan descending a large staircase coming down from the sky. The dream was very vivid and Ryan told her, "It's okay Mom, I'm fine."

Apparently Carol's weirdness was showing through. A year after Ryan died a woman asked Carol's mother, "What's wrong with Carol?" Carol's mother advised the woman that Carol had just lost a son, to which the woman responded, "Well that was a year ago." Sometimes hurt can be compounded by hurt. Not just by painful comments but also by everyday events taken for granted: first day of school, graduation day, birthday, holiday, or day of her son's passing. Carol knew she had to go on with her life. She had other children to care for and she had to be strong for them. She kept Ryan's room the same way he left it for ten years. He had a windup music box in his room and every now and then when Carol cleaned the room the music box would play a couple of notes on it's own. She found comfort in this and took those moments of sound as messages of love from her lost son.

Early on, Carol attended survivor group meetings only to leave the sessions feeling sadder than when she had arrived. She started to go to church and left services feeling the same. She felt she had to put her pain in another place, to set it aside. Not hide it, just properly place it in her mind. There are pictures of Ryan throughout her home. One picture of Ryan sits on a mantel where family photos are taken during holidays. In the back, still very much part of the family, is Ryan appearing in those photographs taken over the years. Carol is an outdoors person who loves hiking, wildlife, and reaching the peaks of various mountains, for it is at these summits where she feels the greatness of life. She recently told me, "Everything I do I enjoy, Ryan lives through me." She also told me that Ryan's death became a benchmark in her life, and views events as either "Before or after Ryan."

Richard Alexander seemed to rally at the hospital but died a few days after the accident, leaving the Alexander family left to grieve with the loss of their son. Clifford and Josh recovered from minor injuries, as did Juha who spent one night in the hospital. Within nine months Juha moved to Finland with his father to be near his mother who was in her native land dying of Parkinson's disease. She passed away within the year and Juha moved back to Ashby with his father. He graduated from high school, went on to become an Emergency Medical Technician, graduated from college with a Degree in Criminal Justice, and in 2009 received a Masters Degree in Business Administration. He lives with his wife and two children on Piper Road in Ashby within a few hundred feet of where his friend Ryan was killed. Juha has come to terms with what happened and visits Ryan's grave now and then. He thinks of his friend often. Band concerts are guaranteed to take him back to that tragic day long ago, as is seeing Ryan's mother.

Ryan is buried at the Glenwood Cemetery in Ashby, which is located halfway between his home and the grammar school he once attended. He rests beneath a gray granite headstone bearing his name, the date he was born, and the date he passed. His parent's names appear just above his, their final dates yet to be inscribed.

In front of North Middlesex Regional High School on Main Street in Townsend, the school Ryan would have attended for his last four years of public education, there is a memorial gazebo. In January of 1999, Elizabeth "Betsie" Hughes and Sean Wellington were killed just a few hundred feet from the front door of the high school. Sean was killed instantly; Betsie died en route to the hospital. They were seniors, high school sweethearts, and scheduled to graduate in just a few months. Irving Chapman was convicted of operating under the influence of alcohol, crossing completely over the centerline while operating a dump truck, and colliding head on with the vehicle Sean was driving. He received an eighteen to twenty-two year prison sentence. Ironically Chapman had pled guilty to misdemeanor motor vehicle homicide in the 1988 death of seventeen-year old Shawn Kinsman, who was also a North Middlesex student. The gazebo was erected shortly after Betsie and Sean were killed, their classmates leading the effort. With the help of locally donated material, money, and labor, the gazebo was completed and dedicated just before graduation. Inside the gazebo there is a plaque entitled "Memorial Gazebo." Just below the following inscription appears, "Dedicated to all victims of youthful and untimely deaths." Meaningful words about good people who left our world far too soon, their numbers far greater than one would suspect unless you were there to witness the tragic losses up close and personal.

That pensive look in Ryan's eyes as he stared back at me from his portrait in the library at Hawthorne Brook Middle School recently seemed to ask, "Do you remember me?" There's an old saying, "Good things happen to good people." If only this were always the case. Sadly bad things happen to good people too. Ryan Lielasus was one of those good people.

# CHAPTER 11

# KELCI FORTUNATO
## FALL 1987

Kelci Fortunato was one of many young people I had the pleasure watching grow up in Townsend. I had attended grammar school with her father and knew her family well. She was by all accounts the typical teenager of the eighties. An attractive young lady with dark hair and an outgoing personality, she was always ready for a jovial comment and just as eager to return one back. She was active in high school, knew how to play seventeen different musical instruments, and performed with the saxophone in the high school marching band. Young, happy, carefree, and always on the go, she epitomized what the American hometown schoolgirl was all about. Kelci graduated from high school in 1984, got married and had a daughter. She would soon separate from her husband and both would go their own way.

Wednesday, November 18, 1987 started out like most others for Kelci. She had just turned twenty-one and was living with her three-year-old daughter at a home she was renting on West Elm Street, in West Townsend. Kelci had three friends visiting her that evening and was talking to another friend on the telephone in the kitchen when her boyfriend came through the front door very upset. He had been drinking and had just been roughed up during an altercation with another guy his age moments before. Kelci remained on the phone while her boyfriend made comments about "getting even" with the guy that just beat him up. With that, he left the kitchen and came back a few moments later waving a handgun while continuing to make threats toward the guy who had just tuned him up. During his rant the gun he was waving around discharged. The bullet struck Kelci in the left frontal lobe of her brain shattering her skull, the projectile fragmenting into many small pieces inside her fractured skullcap. She was immediately rendered unconscious and fell to the floor. The scene was chaotic upon my arrival. The smell of gun smoke hung heavy in the air. In addition to attempting to save Kelci's life, the shooter, as well as other people present, had to be brought under control. The firearm used to shoot Kelci was found by officers in some bushes outside the home, rendered safe, and locked in the trunk of a police vehicle. Emergency medical workers went about the task of attempting to stabilize Kelci. Shortly thereafter, Kelci unconscious and clinging to life, left her home on a stretcher, placed into an awaiting ambulance, and was transported to Burbank Hospital in Fitchburg, Massachusetts nine miles away.

# AFTERMATH:

Police investigation found that the shooting of Kelci Fortunato was accidental. Even though there was wanton disregard for the safety of others, there was no intent on the part of the shooter to actually shoot his victim. There was, however, and still is, a firearms law in Massachusetts that requires anyone in possession of a handgun to be properly licensed. The mandatory sentence for those found in violation is one-year imprisonment. The shooter did not possess this license. Further, he assaulted his victim. In short, he should have known that his irresponsible conduct could, and in this case did, cause injury to another person. Being under the influence of alcohol is not a defense in a criminal act. Maybe in the mind of the offender it is, but as a matter of law it isn't. As such, the shooter was convicted and served one year and four months for the crimes he committed against his "friend." The age-old axiom of being in the wrong place at the wrong time didn't apply in Kelci's shooting. How could it? She was in the right place, her home. How can early evening be considered the wrong time? Unlike the guy who shot her, Kelci was given a much harsher sentence for ironically being in the right place at the right time. Her shooter got just a little over a year while Kelci got a life sentence.

On the evening of November 18, 1987 Kelci arrived at the hospital in Fitchburg and underwent immediate surgery that lasted fourteen hours. She miraculously woke up in the intensive care unit and would spend a total of ten days at Burbank before being transferred to Farnum Rehabilitation Center in Keene, New Hampshire. Kelci's first roommate died shortly after her arrival at Farnum, leaving her to realize just how serious her condition was. She couldn't talk at first and had to learn basic sounds all over again. About two weeks after arriving at rehab her sister Carrie was visiting her. To be expected, Kelci was angry at the situation she found herself in. All she could say to her sister to vent her frustration was the sound "sh." With that Carrie asked, "Do you mean shit?" Kelci nodded her head to indicate yes, to which Carrie replied, "Well that's a start, we can work with that," and the word "shit," as bad as it was, not only became the word of the day, but Kelci's foundation of relearning the language she once knew. She not only had to learn words, she had to relearn some of their meanings, as if starting school all over again. That first attempt to speak a simple four-letter word, as difficult as it was, marked the beginning of the long mental journey of learning how to talk all over again. She would also have to learn how to use her body again as well, for the shooting had left her paralyzed on her right side. After six weeks at the rehabilitation center, Kelci left to go home. In that short period of time she learned to speak in short phrases and how to use a wheelchair. Her road ahead would be a long one.

Kelci would spend the next two years in outpatient speech and occupational therapy. She spent hours developing her tongue to utter sounds much the same as a body builder works with weights to build the body. Having lost the use of the right side of her body, including the use of her right hand, her dominant hand before the shooting, she had to learn how to use her left. She had to be trained how to stand and then to walk again with the use of a cane and braces. She had to deal with an inner anger and often asked herself, "Why me?" A few months after returning home the telephone rang and Kelci answered it as best she could. The caller was the guy who had shot her. He was calling her from prison. She had not heard anything from him and then out of the blue he calls her at home to ask how she was doing. How was she doing? For her to answer that question "not well," would have been an understatement. Kelci had to think about how to answer his question. She knew the answer she wanted to give him but it took time to formulate her five-word answer inside her brain. Constructing a sentence that took only a mere fraction of a second in her mind before her injury now took much longer to accomplish. She had to take the words "ever," "me," "call," "don't," and "again" and put them together in such a way so they made sense to her first before she could say them to him. She had to mentally put them in proper order, have an understanding of each individual word as they stood alone, and then how they related to one another when put together in the form of a sentence. Then came the second difficult part, or the third if you consider the anger within her, she had to speak those five words as best she could, which she finally did. What she said to the guy on the other end was, "Don't ever call me again!" With that she hung up the telephone.

As angry as she was, the "Don't ever call me again!" telephone call proved to be a turning point in her recovery. As soon as she hung up the telephone a new and different five-word sentence formulated in her mind. For some reason, maybe because of the powerful meaning of the message, or perhaps her brain was getting better at playing the word game, whatever the reason, she immediately told herself, "I need to do something." These five words didn't come jumbled and mixed up like the five she had just spoken to her caller. They appeared all at once, all in proper order, and the message was very clear, "I NEED TO DO SOMETHING!"

In the fall of 1989, Kelci, with the aid of a Pell Grant, entered college locally and then transferred to Prince George's Community College in Largo, Maryland in 1991. Her daughter remained living at home with Kelci's mother while she pursued her education. She bounced around during the beginning, living on welfare and living with roommates to cut costs. Kelci didn't know if there was such a thing as living on "easy street," but she knew what living on "difficult street" was all about, because that was where she had been residing since November 18, 1987. She eventually left Prince George's and continued to bounce around. In 1994 she transferred her college credits, along with herself, to the University of Maryland and graduated from there in 1997 with a Bachelor's Degree in English. She didn't want to teach and she couldn't find a job. She continued to live on welfare and with roommates. She constantly interviewed for jobs. She wasn't allowed to keep her driver's license because she suffered a traumatic brain injury. Everything she attempted to do had to be accessible by bus, and often felt grateful for the Washington Metropolitan Area Transit Authority, for without it she couldn't travel anywhere. Her world was governed by where the metro system went. She eventually got a job in Washington, D.C. and lived in Laurel, Maryland with roommates to keep her housing costs down. Her work evolved around conducting research into "How To Do Chores" for a children's website; how to clean your room easier and so forth. All of this was short-lived when the company she was working at folded in 2000. With that Kelci went back to Prince George's Community College and pursued website design. She became very active at college taking four to five classes per semester and became Editor-in-Chief of the college's newspaper. She got married on June 25, 2002 and went on to graduate in 2003. She didn't stop, however. She went back to Prince George's and earned her third degree in computer programming, graduating in 2005. In 2010 she started her own company, Feeney Designs L.L.C., which designs websites for small businesses and authors. Her husband, retired from the military, pilots unmanned drones.

Recently Kelci told me something quite profound by saying, "My getting shot was just a hiccup, really." I was taking notes at the time and asked her to stop for a moment so I could totally take that statement in. A hiccup? How could someone so gravely and wrongfully injured consider what had happened to her so trivial? A mere "hiccup!" She went on to tell me that she could get depressed and sometimes does, but she continues to keep very busy. The hardest time for her is on the anniversary date of her shooting, for it triggers the event that so dramatically changed her life. She often "loses it" on this day and just sits on the floor and cries. She does not remember the shooting but has lived with it every day since. Kelci differentiates between her mind and her brain by saying her brain is simply an organ of her body that surgeons worked on when she was shot. Her mind goes far beyond that, for she alone controls her thinking. For her it's a mind versus brain game that she manages. She not only lives by a set rules for the game she plays, she has made many of them up. The evasiveness of her injury demands that she does not consume alcohol, so she doesn't. Perhaps it goes much deeper than that, for Kelci has fought hard everyday to regain the use of her mind. Why would she risk losing control over something she has worked so hard to get back? She, if anyone, knows firsthand the damage that the misuse of alcohol can bring. For Kelci the mind game goes on. The good news, she's winning.

# CHAPTER 12

# ANDREW GUSTAFSON
## DECEMBER 1987

Andrew Gustafson grew up with good parents and a brother and sister in West Brookfield, Massachusetts during the early nineteen-fifties into the early seventies. He attended school, church, Sunday school, and did those adventurous things that boys do growing up. At an early age, for reasons he cannot fully explain, he developed an interest in God and his teachings, even though religion was not forced upon him at home. On Christmas Eve 1965, at age 12, Andy's sister Susan gave him a Bible within which God's words were printed in red while the remaining text appeared in black. Andy was intrigued by this gift. He would read the Bible regularly along with other books required for his public school education. He graduated from Quaboag Regional High School in 1971. Priscilla Morgan, a pretty girl with dark hair, attended the same regional high school. She was one year behind Andy and on occasion they would exchange casual greetings in the hallways. Priscilla graduated from high school in 1972 and went on to attend Worcester State College (now Worcester State University), the same college Andy started attending the year before. Andy became a friendly face in a college crowd of strangers for Priscilla, and their friendship grew. They started dating and soon became sweethearts. Andy graduated from Worcester State a year ahead of Priscilla and continued with his education at Boston Law School. The love that Priscilla and Andy had for each other grew stronger over time and Priscilla's father, Reverend Bill Morgan, joined them in marriage on August 21, 1975 in a traditional wedding ceremony at the First Congregational Church in Great Barrington,

Massachusetts. On their marriage license Priscilla listed her occupation as "sales clerk," while Andy listed his as "student." Although Priscilla had graduated with a degree in teaching she was unable to find a job in her chosen profession. The American economy was in a severe downswing, budgets were cut in both the private and public sectors, and there weren't many jobs available. In order to support her husband through law school Priscilla sold shoes. They lived in a rented three-decker in Worcester, Massachusetts during their early financially-lean years. Andy graduated from Boston College of Law in 1978 and was admitted to the Massachusetts Bar that same year. They bought their first home in Ashby, Massachusetts and within a few years purchased a home in Townsend, and started their family. They were devoted to one another as well as to their faith, and attended the Townsend Congregational Church regularly. Their family grew to three with the addition of their daughter Abigail, born December 8, 1979, and then to four with the birth of their son William on November 12, 1982.

On the morning of December 1, 1987 Andrew Gustafson woke up a very happy man and enjoyed eating breakfast with his two children alongside his wife, now three months pregnant. His daughter Abigail, one week shy of her eighth birthday would leave home for Spaulding Memorial School later in the morning, wearing her blue and yellow S.M.S. tee shirt. His son William, age five, dressed in light green OshKosh coveralls, would spend most of his day with his mom. Adding to his happiness, Andy would be closing on a major business deal later in the day, one he had been working on for months. One that would bring further financial security to his family. For Andy, life couldn't get any better. His home was filled with a sense of Christian love that was growing in leaps and bounds. Laughter, hugs, and kisses were common occurrences around the Gustafson household. Later that same evening Andrew Gustafson arrived back home to share his happy day with his family. His joy immediately turned to horrific grief when he entered his home to find that his wife had been murdered. His life stopped at this moment. He didn't know it at the time but his two children were also deceased, drowned fully clothed in separate bathtubs. Responding police would find their bodies while searching the home shortly after their arrival.

I arrived at the Gustafson home shortly thereafter. One of the first tasks I encountered was to eliminate Andy as a suspect in the killing of his family. A family member, or someone very close to the victim, is responsible for approximately seventy-five percent of the people murdered in the United States each year. As such my task was to either eliminate him as a suspect, or start to build a case against him based upon my observations of the crime scene, and more importantly at this juncture, of him. My findings would be critical in setting the course of the investigation. I interviewed Andy less than two hours after the murders were discovered at the end of his driveway in the company of his parents who were there to support him. Not just emotionally, but physically as well, as each held an arm while he stood facing me. I watched Andy closely as I spoke. I studied his demeanor. I physically checked his clothing and exposed skin for any indication of blood or gunshot residue. His wife had just been shot in the head with a small caliber weapon after being tied spread eagle with rope to the four corners of her bed. A later autopsy would show she had been sexually assaulted and shot twice at close range. I observed Andy's expressions, his movements, his eyes, his hands, and how he verbally responded to my questions. His two children had just been drowned in separate bathtubs and held in their positions of doom by someone much larger and stronger than they were. I paid particular attention to his feet, lower pants, and sleeves. He was wearing a business suit, tie, and white shirt complete with topcoat. The same clothing he had on when he left his house that morning for work. All appeared normal with no sign of disarray, staining, or wetness. Before this tragedy I had heard the death moans of many people during their last moments of life and Andy presented this same mournful sound to my seasoned ear while attempting to answer my simple questions. People I found making this noise at the end of their lives were most often lying in a prone position or upside down entangled in wreckage.

Andy was different in the sense that we were standing facing one another. I made eye contact with him often but there was nothing there. His mouth uttered hard to distinguish sounds, which meant either yes or no, but sounded very much the same except for tone variation. His answers of more than one word seemed to blend into one agonizing sound. The vacancy within his mind was apparent; his eyes weren't speaking to me. He was by all accounts a dead man standing, yet still able to utter sounds. I know no better way to describe the dreadful moans being emitted from his body or the nothingness in his eyes. He was under my investigative microscope but I doubt he understood what I was attempting to accomplish even though he was a seasoned attorney. Within minutes the image of a broken man became very apparent to me. I had been speaking to someone with a shattered spirit, not a killer.

I left Andy with his parents and went back to his house, now a major crime scene, and reported to Middlesex County First Assistant District Attorney Thomas Reilly that Andrew Gustafson was not our man. Murders committed in Massachusetts come under the immediate jurisdiction of the Office of the District Attorney in the county where the crime was committed and Reilly was the main man to go to. Based upon my opinion our investigation changed focus away from Andrew Gustafson. At my request an army of over one hundred uniformed state police troopers arrived in Townsend to ease the fear that the community was gripped in, as well as conduct active roadblocks in search for information. The entire Middlesex County State Police Homicide Unit, under the direction of lead investigator Trooper Robert Long, went to work immediately and was backed up by the entire Middlesex County State Police Drug Enforcement Unit. I added two Townsend officers to this group, Erving Marshall and David Kumpu, to provide input and information about people within the community. This extended group of investigators developed a short list of people of interest with respect to the murders and the task force fanned out to talk with these people. One of the names on the list was Daniel LaPlante, age seventeen, and an adult by

Massachusetts's criminal standards. When two state troopers went to his home to talk to him about forty-eight hours after the murders he ran into the woods behind his home. This triggered a major manhunt. We were faced with the possibility of a mass murderer on the loose and Long, Reilly, and I decided it best to provide his photo to the news media as a person of interest, but more important, if in fact LaPlante was our man, to get his picture out for the public to see and be warned. At the time we didn't know how important this decision would become. Shortly thereafter LaPlante broke into a home in Pepperell, Massachusetts, where he took a sixteen-year-old girl hostage at gunpoint and forced her into the family car and drove off. Unbeknownst to her assailant, the girl had just seen LaPlante's picture on the front page of the newspaper and knew the danger she was facing. At the first traffic light she jumped from the vehicle, ran to the nearest home, and alerted police. Within seventy-two hours after the murders LaPlante was taken into custody during the evening hours of December 4th. He was convicted the following October for committing one of the most heinous crimes in recent Massachusetts' history and sentenced to life in prison without the possibility of parole.

I have purposely avoided penning the details of the Gustafson crime scene as best possible or the particulars relative to the ensuing trial. Rather than sensationalize how a mother and her two children were viciously murdered, I have elected to show how one man, a loving husband and father, survived this terrible tragedy. How he continued to keep himself going in mind, spirit, and body after such horrific loss.

# AFTERMATH:

On December 5th, mourners led by Andy Gustafson tearfully filled the Townsend Congregational Church to say goodbye to the Gustafson family. There were so many people in attendance, the overflow stood outside in the cold morning air. Priscilla had taught at the Townsend Cooperative Playschool in the basement of the church. The same one her son Billy attended. Abby had sung a solo in this house of worship just two weeks before. Young parents sat with their children in their laps. Midway through the service, which lasted about thirty-five minutes, Andy rose from his seat to deliver the eulogy for his family. "Never ever say this was God's will. I know that God is crying and mourning too." This was the first time Andy had spoken publicly since the murders and he continued on about the love he had for his family and they for him, "a love so strong, so deep, that it can never be taken away." The once loving Priscilla, Abby, and Billy, now silenced in death, lay before him. This would be his last moment with the three people closest to his heart. He wasn't able to hold them close anymore, so he embraced them, as best he could, with words of love. Struggling to keep his composure Andy continued, "Every day we kissed each other, and hugged each other, and told each other we loved each other. It could never have been better because it was the best. Our love is stronger than any hate of evil." In conclusion Andy said, "I love you all," and then with tears in his eyes, stepped down from the pulpit.

Townsend changed after the Gustafson murders. Doors that were normally left unlocked were never left that way again. The community was blanketed in disbelief, sorrow, and anger. The once relaxed lifestyle of a small town changed overnight from carefree to careful. People who normally looked ahead to the future started to look back over their shoulder. Major news networks descended upon Townsend and the Gustafson news tragedy went nationwide. Beneath all the hype away from the crowd Andy Gustafson sat alone with his own unbelievable disbelief, sorrow, and anger. He was locked inside himself, oblivious at first to the love and support that his family and church community continued to bestow upon him. In the medical profession numbing agents are administered to ease pain. Andy was a living contradiction of this medical practice, for his pain and numbness coexisted as partners, not adversaries. They fed off one another, growing day after day. Andy would endure months of legal maneuvering as the criminal justice system moved slowly forward. He had lost his family and each new day brought further grief. As the case progressed through the legal system new details would be brought forth and either printed in the press or broadcast over the major news networks. Where does someone in Andy's terrible circumstance find the strength to go on? To understand the answer to that question you have to get to know Andy, for he is the only person that can answer it.

Andy would tell you that he survived for many reasons. He had two loving parents who taught him, as well as his brother and sister, right from wrong, and was raised accordingly. His parents believed in the word of God, and in the process of growing up, he learned through his faith that there was evil in the world as well. He credits his parents for providing him with a strong moral foundation, which ultimately prepared him for what he would have to endure. He also credits Priscilla and her parents for continuing to support his already established strong social compass. His own ongoing exploration of the Bible from an early age proved to be his anchor in the face of nature's greatest fury. A biblical verse from Matthew he read in the bible his sister gave him long ago about the wise man who built his house on stone, and the foolish man who built his on sand, and when the strong rains came the house built on sand was washed away, proved to be prophetic. He learned and believed early on to follow the word of Matthew and to build his life on a strong foundation, so he could weather any storm that came his way. Over and over the word of Matthew and those he loved most remained in the forefront of his thoughts. Andy told me the Gospel excerpt from John, Chapter 1 held him up when he started to fall, and recited it to me without hesitation recently as we sat together all these years later. "The light shines in the darkness and the darkness has not overcome it." He recalls thinking of this verse while walking in the rain shortly after losing his family and thinking God was crying with him. His God hadn't left him to cry alone.

During the first four months after the loss of his family Andy wavered from his religious beliefs and contemplated taking his own life. This, he felt, would end his nightmare and reunite him with his lost family. The reason he couldn't do it was because he couldn't hurt the family he still had, those closest to him who had taught him to be strong by understanding and practicing the word of God. He also realized that he would die someday and eventually be reunited with Priscilla, Abigail, and William anyway. Sometime between four and five months after he lost his wife and two children Andy walked outside one morning and realized the sun was shining. Something that had been going on day after day, but something he hadn't noticed. This first new glimpse of sunshine paused him to stop and take notice. He looked around in astonishment. How many days of sunshine had he missed? He felt guilty for having lost touch with the real world around him. There must have been some good days. How many? He wasn't sure. He had been lost in such deep depression he didn't even notice the sun come up, let alone shine. Days of darkness had grown into months of nothingness, so black, so void of any meaning, it totally isolated him from the living world around him. His first realization of the sun shining was his very first step in attempting to take back control of his life. It was a small step, a very small step, one that took months to achieve, but a step in the right direction. There would be many setbacks too, but he didn't measure the steps back the same as he did the ones he took forward. In his mind three steps back could be overcome by just one step forward, for it wasn't the absolute value of the number that mattered, it was the direction the number took him that counted most.

Andy avoided the use of alcohol and credits his religious faith for giving him the strength to avoid temptation. He couldn't read a newspaper or watch the news on television. Every night he would be a guest at a different home in town for dinner. He will tell you that his Congregational Church community supported him as an extension of his own family, as did the Townsend community at large. One of the many acts of kindness bestowed upon him was receiving handmade cards from a third grade class along with a note from the Catholic nun who taught them. He was deeply moved by such an outpouring of love from children. There were many other acts of compassion. Each one was something he could hold on to much like a mountain climber holds onto a tiny outcropping of rock to prevent the inevitable. For Andy was attempting to scale a precipice not many are required to climb in life. He was in a dangerous situation and he knew it. His faith in God told him to continue on but the difficult journey upward remained a struggle. For him the key was to keep moving up. Some days there would be setbacks when all that was gained would be lost. Triggers that caused his mind to lose focus were endless; children outside playing, a mother holding a child, a happy family together, and the list went on and on. Sometimes there were moments that stretched into hours, when all he could do was desperately hold on. One failed grasp and all would be lost.

In the months that followed his "sunshine revelation," Andy would often walk through the cemetery. He found comfort visiting his deceased family there, knowing they were in a peaceful place. Knowing he was close to them. He found solace in his quiet walks and eventually noticed the gravestones of other children buried there, and grew to understand other people had faced tragedy too. During one of these quiet times he pondered how he could think God was good to him when God had let bad things happen to his family and to him. Did that mean God was a bad God? Ironically he found the answer within a core belief established long before the tragedy happened, in the realization that what had happened to him and his family wasn't the work of God, but that of an evil spirit. He attended survivor support group meetings and grew to learn that he wasn't the only spouse or parent that suffered as a "secondary victim" and found strength in strangers brought together by tragedy. I was taken by his use of the expression "secondary victim," and found comfort in his conscious acknowledgement that he had moved away from the appalling state of being the "primary victim" he once was, not that there is much difference between the two in his case. I had this sense that he was telling me he doesn't live with his nightmare moment-to-moment as he once did, but more on a day-to-day basis. A sign that healing within his mind and heart was still ongoing even after twenty-four years have passed. Time passes, but time does not erase. Invisible scars forever remain, deeply embedded and permanently etched upon the mind. Solitary sores that sometime fester with the slightest provocation to open up the old wound. During the first and second year after the tragedy Andy would look at photos of his family and tremble while he cried. There are also home movies he has yet to look at and doubts he ever will. Andy focuses on the today of his life knowing full well his yesterdays are forever gone.

Andy understood at an early age through his religious teachings that he lived in a world of good verses evil, one that challenged his sense of righteousness. He never heard God actually talk to him after he lost his family. There was never a miraculous revelation, never a bright flash of light, but he knew from God's teachings that he had to be strong and develop a new direction in his life. He constantly reminded himself that he couldn't live alone and shut out the world around him, the dark world he grew to know so well during the first months after his loss. The one in which the sun never shone. He knew he had to develop a focused meaning for life, his life, and sought sound direction through prayer. He became close to Carol Seaver, a member of his church who had lost her husband to cancer. Andy and Carol had known each other for years and their shared loss brought them closer together. In 1989 they were married and shortly thereafter they adopted two children, Laura and Holly. Four lives once broken were starting to be put back together.

As hard as it was for Andy to accept, he knew there was nothing he could do for the wife, daughter, and son he had lost. Unable to change that, he decided to give back and help other children as best he could. In 1992 he became an advocate for children in need of legal help by making his lawyer-self available to them via the

Massachusetts Committee for Public Counsel Services. In addition to being a good husband and father, Andy went on to represent hundreds of children brought into the courtroom. Many were there for no other reason than being a child in need of someone to help them. To protect them from further harm, to let them feel an arm around their shoulder, and to let them know that they weren't alone. Especially those caught up in situations over which they had little or no control, at an age when life should be full of joy and promise rather than horrific unknowns. These kids didn't know it but they had one tremendous advocate. The guy that represented them fully understood what being alone and desperate felt like. He had been there. He knew what it was like to live in a world without sunshine. Andy would continue to provide rays of hope for kids until 2004. In an attempt to give back to his faith he left the judicial system and became an Associate Conference Minister for Stewardship and Financial Development with the Massachusetts Conference of the United Church of Christ, which he continues today.

Andy and Carol still live in Townsend, two doors down from the Congregational Church, the same church they have been attending for years. Their daughters Laura and Holly have grown up and graduated from college. Andy recently told me that there is nothing unique about the person he is. He considers himself no different than any other man. He was brought into a personal tragic event not of his choosing, yet he arrived with a strong foundation based on his faith. His religious teachings keep coming back to him, and he will tell you earth isn't more like heaven because of our own choosing, not God's. He is convinced our world would be a better place if people got out of themselves and cared more about others, yet strongly believes that it is not his role to judge his fellow man, and reaffirmed his belief that there is hope and possibility for everyone. He finds strength in his wife, family, his church community, and the one person that has embraced him all of his life, God. He still has the Bible his sister gave to him almost fifty years ago.

Priscilla, Abigail, and William Gustafson are buried next to one another at the Hillside cemetery in Townsend. On the front of their headstone at the base, the following Biblical passage from John 1:5 is inscribed; "THE LIGHT SHINES IN THE DARKNESS AND THE DARKNESS HAS NOT OVERCOME IT." On the reverse side the following appears; "A LIFE LIKE THEIRS HAS LEFT A RECORD SWEET FOR MEMORY TO DWELL UPON." Just below their individual names embedded in stone is a reading from Corinthians 13:8, "LOVE NEVER DIES."

# CHAPTER 13

## CHELSEA ADAMS
### WINTER 1989

Shortly before nine o'clock on Sunday morning, December 17, 1989 I received a telephone call at my home from my communications center advising me to go to the Adams home at 398 Main Street in West Townsend. The police officer there was requesting my assistance relative to a deceased child at that location. I immediately grabbed my briefcase and headed to the Adams home. I knew there was a sick child living there and arrived within fifteen minutes.

Anne Adams, who was holding her daughter Chelsea cradled in her arms, met me at the door. I could clearly see that Chelsea, who was just two months shy of her second birthday, was deceased. Anne was seven and a half months pregnant with her sixth child and lived on Main Street with her husband and four other children. Chelsea had been born with myelomeningocele spina bifida. In individuals with myelomeningocele, the infused portion of the spinal column allows the spinal cord to protrude through an opening. The meningeal membranes that cover the spinal cord form a sac enclosing the spinal elements. In this type of spina bifida, the involved area is represented by a flattened, plate-like mass of nervous tissue with no overlying membrane. The exposure of these nerves and tissues make a baby more prone to life-threatening infections. In short, the protruded portion of the spinal cord and the nerves, at whatever level of the spinal cord afflicted, are damaged or not properly developed. Thus, the higher the level of the defect in the spine, the more severe the associated nerve dysfunction and resultant paralysis. Unfortunately

Chelsea's spina bifida was not only in the more common lower spinal area, but her upper spine as well. Having an opening in the lower spine area, above the tailbone, is the most common type of defect and generally affects bowel and bladder control, and often walking ability. These problems can usually be controlled with catheters and braces and don't sentence the otherwise healthy child to an early death. Chelsea, not only had this more common type, but she was also born with the condition in her upper spine, which immediately threatened to take her life. She remained in the hospital for the first three months of her life battling her afflictions. Anne would drive thirty-five miles one way twice each day, bringing her four-year-old son Jake with her in the mornings to see her. The hospital staff felt it best that Chelsea remained hospitalized but Anne was determined to bring her daughter home, and had to fight to do it. She fought to love her daughter in a way that only a mother can. To make her part of the Adams' family. She had to learn how to properly care for a child that required constant medical attention. Anne's family had to do the same. Even Jake, as young as he was, knew how to properly set Chelsea's oxygen at level three. Together mother, family, and Chelsea were up for the fight, and together they would battle Chelsea's affliction for the rest of her very short life.

Chelsea came home after her first three months on earth to a family that loved her. Her first year passed as best possible for someone in her condition. Constant care became the norm. In-home nursing care, oxygen therapy, airway suctioning, and feeding tubes became a way of life. Resuscitation and asphyxiation became words Anne had to know and understand even though she wished they never existed. Attention to her daughter's condition was constant. During Chelsea's second year her condition worsened. She had undergone a dozen surgeries before she was twenty months old. The most serious was to her upper spine and brain to help ease her inability to swallow. This complex and dangerous surgery unfortunately did not improve her ability to swallow, a function necessary for her to properly eat and breathe. As a result of this failed attempt her gastrointestinal tube remained her only means of nourishment. Her ability to breathe properly did not improve either, and she would often gag and appear as if she were drowning. On many occasions Chelsea would stop breathing and look at Anne in desperation. Eyes popped wide open and staring out in what is known as the "drowning expression." How hard this must have been for a child not quite two years old who didn't know what drowning meant. Couldn't understand what was going on. These "close call" events were always followed by a beautiful smile from a cute little girl who may not have understood her affliction but was determined to beat it. Prone to infection, Chelsea developed pneumonia four times during her last year and went back and forth to the hospital. Anne continued to give her daughter the love that every child needs. Took her to McDonald's even though she required a feeding tube to eat. Packed up all her medical equipment and took her along with the rest of the family for vacation on Cape Cod. Showered her daily with warmth and love.

I entered the Adams' home and walked with Anne and Chelsea into their living room. We sat and talked for a few minutes, our conversation centering on Chelsea at first. How she had been born with spina bifida and how Chelsea's case was more severe than most as the top of her spine failed to close completely, where in most cases this condition was most often found at the base of the spine. Sadly, Chelsea had been born with both. We sat and talked about how beautiful Chelsea looked. I could sense I was in the presence of a mother who didn't want to let go of a child she deeply loved. I had been in this situation before but had encountered it mostly in cases of sudden infant death syndrome. Even in homes after delivering death notifications to parents there was always an element of disbelief. Some mothers remained very quiet but their eyes spoke of an unwillingness to accept. Anne's eyes and actions were different in the sense she knew her daughter was gone. Like any other mother, she didn't want to accept that fact, but she had to, and she had to do it with extraordinary strength for the sake of her remaining children. As such, she told me she understood I had a job to do, but asked if I could do what I had to do with as little impact as possible on her family. She wanted her children to remember Chelsea's death as a peaceful event. Avoiding any additional commotion, such as flashing lights and sirens, would be deeply appreciated. I told Anne there wouldn't be any further noticeable police response, but there could be a couple of investigators out to assist me if necessary.

I felt deep compassion for this mother now caught up in such a tragic event, but I was also employed to investigate deaths, especially those classified as "untimely." The General Laws of the Commonwealth of Massachusetts dictate that all suspicious or untimely deaths come under the jurisdiction of the District Attorney within the county where the death occurred, as well the Office of Chief Medical Examiner. At the very least I was required to immediately contact these two offices and advise them as to what I was doing whenever I became involved in any death. I took stalk of the surroundings and noted the medical equipment within the home. I also knew that Chelsea had been very sick and struggled to survive. I dismissed the uniformed officer that had arrived at the home before me and used the Adams' telephone to make two calls. The first was to the Massachusetts State Police Crime Prevention and Control Unit. A small group of state police officers attached to the Middlesex County District Attorney's Office to assist in the investigation of untimely deaths. In short, the "homicide squad." I told the on-duty trooper whom I had worked with on other cases about the circumstances of Chelsea's death and felt that I did not need further assistance. He agreed and asked that I forward my report once I had completed my investigation. I then called Doctor Lawrence Churchville II, Medical Examiner within my jurisdiction. Massachusetts's law also dictates that a human body subject to police investigation cannot be moved to an authorized receiving facility without the medical examiners approval. Doctor Churchville lived in Townsend; we had worked many cases together and had developed a strong professional relationship. I told him the circumstances surrounding Chelsea's death and he authorized me to remove Chelsea's body from the home to the funeral home of the parent's choice. Professional relationships, just like those of a personal nature, evolve around trust, which grows as the relationship develops. As such, I was given absolute authority over the investigation into the death of Chelsea Adams by making two telephone calls. There would be no further outside intrusion at the Adams home.

I walked back into the living room and asked Anne questions I needed to complete my report and then advised her I had received permission to have Chelsea taken to the funeral home of her choice. We sat and talked for a few minutes more. I could sense by her tears that Anne was realizing her time with Chelsea was running out. If only she could stretch one more minute into another. If only she could capture time and fast freeze their final moment together and make it last. As difficult as it was to accept, Anne knew death wouldn't allow that. She sat for another moment and then walked into the kitchen where she undressed Chelsea and started to give her a bath in a baby tub in the kitchen sink. Something she had done many times before, but this would be the last time. I helped as best I could. I was taken by the remarkable courage of this mother. Bathing her daughter with her silent tears slowly running down her cheeks into the bath water below. She had often bathed her daughter with love. This time it was different. This time, the last time, she bathed her in her tears. I could feel my eyes welling and did my best to maintain my professional composure. I knew the final family portrait of peace and love Anne was trying so hard to create, far be it from me to destroy that image. I found my strength in Anne and held back my tears as best I could. After she had washed and dried her daughter, Anne dressed Chelsea in what was to be her second year Christmas outfit, complete with topcoat, hat, and shiny black shoes. I called the Anderson Funeral Home and requested someone meet us there as soon as possible. The Adams children, Sarah 15, Leslie 13, Meghan 10, and Jake now 6, all kissed their sister goodbye in a very peaceful yet tear-filled parting. From a distance one would assume that Chelsea was simply asleep in her mother's arms, which she was, but not as it appeared. Chelsea had crossed over to the other side and was now in an eternal sleep. Dressed for the cold outside I left the Adams home with Carl, Chelsea's dad, carrying her all bundled up in her new outfit. Anne gave her daughter a last kiss. I held the door for Carl as he got into my unmarked police cruiser with Chelsea in his arms, and then the three of us drove out of the driveway headed for the funeral home. From every outward appearance just three people simply headed for church.

# AFTERMATH:

Anne Adams delivered her sixth child on schedule and named her Cheyenne. Anne still lives in the same home on Main Street in Townsend where Chelsea passed away. She recently told me, "When I lost Chelsea I became a member of a terrible club I wish I didn't belong." To fully grasp that statement two conditions must exist. First, you must have a child, and second, the horrible part, you must lose your child to death. There's no trying it for a day to see how it feels. There's no imagining it. In fact there is no way to understand the depth of that feeling until you are required to live it day after day. There are no "time outs." Membership in the "terrible club" lasts forever. You don't have to be reminded to pay your dues. Once you become a member you pay them daily. Whenever asked, Anne will say she has six children, not five. Chelsea remains very much alive in her mind and heart. Anne's other five children have all grown up and remain close to their mom.

Chelsea sleeps alongside Avenue 7 in the Hillside Cemetery in Townsend under a heart-shaped headstone that bares her name, Chelsea Sabrina Adams. The dates of her short life are included just below her name and on the back the following epitaph appears: "IF ONLY WE COULD HOLD YOU AND HUG YOU YET AWHILE, GOD CALLED HIS SWEETEST ANGEL HOME BECAUSED HE

MISSED HER SMILE – MOMMY." Unquestionably this is not a story with a happy ending. When you move beyond the tragic tale told you soon realize Chelsea's story is not over. She lives on in the hearts of many, especially those who grew to love her. She will be remembered for many reasons. Chelsea's legacy is ongoing. She continues to be one of our littlest great teachers. If ever we have one of those moments when life throws us a curve, when we feel the bottom has fallen out and we struggle to continue on, Chelsea Adams might be someone to turn to for a lesson in survival. In the face of life-threatening adversity she smiled! Shouldn't we all?

I feel obligated to pass along this most important lesson in self-preservation, taught to me by a child much bigger than life and her mother, a woman of incredible strength. Two people I formed a psychological bond with on December 17, 1989; one a mother, the other her child, both possessing enormous strength.

# CHAPTER 14

# WILLIAM MAY
## SPRING 1990

I had been on the job for over seventeen years. In addition to police work I had volunteered the first ten years of my career working on the municipal ambulance service. I had witnessed a vast number of human tragedies. Between both police and ambulance services I had performed cardiopulmonary resuscitation (CPR) on many people: friends, children, parents of friends, and complete strangers. I could count my success in those cases on one hand. I had investigated a suicide where an adult male, who I knew, laid face up on his bed and used both hands to drive a hunting knife into his chest and through his heart. Something I didn't think humanly possible, only to investigate another similar suicide involving the father of a friend a few years later. Not counting Randy's warning shot, I had been fired upon twice; both at night by intoxicated males, which may have worked in my favor, for both, missed their target. Me! I had been awarded the Silver Star for Bravery by the National Federation of Police Officers for successfully taking down an armed suspect holding an undercover state trooper and myself at gunpoint. This too was another nighttime event.

On December 26, 1986 I responded to a serious head-on motor vehicle accident on rural Route 13 just north of town. A family had left their home in southern New Hampshire to visit relatives in Worcester, Massachusetts for a post-Holiday celebration. They were traveling in two vehicles. The father and one child in one vehicle followed by the mother and their other two children in a second one. I arrived at the crash site quite quickly and immediately assessed the condition of the victims. The scene soon became very busy with respective first responders doing what had to be done. The lone occupant of the other vehicle involved was dead and wedged up under her dashboard. I would later learn that she was a mother and a grandmother who was loved by many. The eighteen-year-old front female passenger in the family vehicle was also dead, killed instantly from a fracture of her cervical spine. Her mother, trapped behind the steering wheel next to her, was successfully extricated from the wreckage but succumbed to her injuries while being transported to the hospital. Her five-year-old son, sitting in the back on the passenger side, suffered fractures but was conscious and alert when he left the scene in an ambulance. While all this was going on, the father realizing his wife was no longer behind him, waited a few minutes and then doubled back to see if there was some type of problem. I held him in my arms as he dropped to his knees after I told him his eighteen-year-old daughter was deceased within the wreckage of their car.

I had attended an autopsy at Worcester Memorial Hospital in December of 1986 relative to a case I was working on. At another examining table there was the body of a teenage male who had either jumped or fallen from the ninth floor of a building in Worcester. Aside from being a good-looking young man with dark hair, what struck me was the multiple compound impact fractures to his legs. His personal effects were laid out on the table as well, and there were illicit drugs within his belongings. I didn't know the full particulars involved with his death, but asked myself, "Why? What went so wrong? What led someone so young, so strong, and so good looking to end up at the morgue at Worcester Memorial? Was this young man's death a suicide or did drugs push him over the edge, or in his case, off? Maybe in his distorted mind, if in fact it was, did he simply think he could walk from the top of one building to another?" I had studied the medical and legal ramifications of death at the University of Massachusetts Medical School in Worcester, and remembered examining a case where a young female high on hallucinogenic drugs felt she could actually do this and fell twelve stories to her death. So that was a possibility. I had investigated approximately fifty suicides, and had participated in many autopsies, because I attended those for other causes of death as well. I found I could conditionally accept deaths of older people depending upon cause, but when I got up close and personal with those who died young I couldn't totally process those cases to a final conclusion in my mind, even though the case files were eventually closed. I always held fast to the belief that death was part of the cycle of life starting at birth, then followed by infancy, childhood, adolescence, maturing, adulthood, aging, and for each of us, death. I had trouble trying to come to terms with the shorter cycles of human existence: infancy to death, childhood to death, adolescence to death, and maturing to death. I had seen so many lives prevented from completing full life cycles in a town that was so peaceful and idyllic when I grew up there. Maybe all this went on when I was growing up, and if it did, I was oblivious to most of it at the time. Now this. My hometown was not what it once was to me. Now what? In June of 1989 I lost the best friend I ever had when my father passed away. The one person I could go to knowing his advice would be without any ulterior motive and given to me with compassionate understanding. I would visit his grave almost daily and eat my lunch there with him, just the two of us. I even talked to him. I didn't know it at the time but within a few months I would find myself in serious medical trouble.

By October of 1989 I was restless. My workload was heavy. The economy had faltered and I was preparing budget after budget trying to cope with rising costs and falling tax revenues. Budget preparation was time consuming. During a normal year I would only have to prepare one. I had a host of other administrative duties to perform along with uniformed duties on the street. In police work time is critical, especially within the first hour of a medical emergency or the first forty-eight hours after a major crime was committed. I knew all about time management. I just didn't have enough time to manage, or staff. Funding requests for additional help were voted down, not for reasons that weren't recognized, there just wasn't any available money within the town's limited tax structure. Financial conditions worsened and instead of adding staff I had to let officers go. Easy to do on paper perhaps, but when you stop someone's livelihood you worry about his or her survival. They had families too. I had hired each of them, but they never worked for me, they worked with me. I was good at what I did because of the people that surrounded me. Clearly without all of them my job became far more difficult than before.

The department, which took years to build, was cut in half within a period of two years. As a result, many cases were simply recorded into the daily log and not investigated! Since 1984 I had been trying to convince taxpayers to build a new police station and was met with frustration after frustration. Fighting for money that wasn't available was just as difficult as working out of a police station that didn't exist. Nonetheless I felt duty-bound to my community, and especially to those who worked directly with me, to provide a secure police facility. I would go to bed at night and couldn't sleep, and when I did, I would dream. My conscious thoughts would bounce from one thing to another. Could I have presented my budget better? Clearer? Did I do all that I could have done for this person? That person? Could I have prevented this from happening? Or that? When I finally drifted off to sleep, some of my subconscious thoughts took me back to former gruesome events presenting images in the present, not the past.

My father's death was heavy on my mind when Chelsea Adams came into my life in December 1989 because of her untimely death. Although her death was medically anticipated her passing was premature, and in my mind, terribly unfair. Certainly her shortened life cycle was on my mind, and I couldn't stop thinking about how difficult it must have been for someone like Chelsea, who hadn't even approached the age of reason, to struggle the way she did, and through it all, smile! The 1987 Gustafson murder case had been ongoing, continuing through 1988, until a conviction was obtained on October 25th, while various appeals continued after that. The 1986

Christmas crash that killed three people headed to holiday festivities with other family members was heavy on my mind too. What kept coming back to me was the blonde-colored hair of the eighteen-year-old girl killed that day. I had immediately noticed her hair color when I first went inside the wreckage to check her condition. To gain access to her I had to enter the vehicle from the rear, which at first obscured her face because it was pointed down and away from me. I had a daughter of the same age and appearance. For an instant I thought of my own child inside the wreckage. For that split second of time I felt guilty thinking of my own when I was supposed to be focused on the victim. Clearly she was deceased. How does a father accept and then *dead* *?* manage such tremendous unspeakable loss? I had gone to the local funeral home later that day to have the young lady's remains positively identified by an aunt and uncle, and the sadness of that moment lingered in my mind. The uncle, in his middle forties, reeked with the smell of alcohol. I prepared both parties by telling them their niece was resting on a table under a white sheet. I further explained that once aside the table I would raise the sheet so they could look at her face and advise me if the person was in fact their niece. I also advised them we could take our time once inside if they so desired. We entered the room, I raised the sheet, and they made a positive identification. I left the victim's face exposed while they stood and talked to the deceased, telling her how much they loved her. Not an uncommon occurrence. We lingered there for about ten minutes until they both kissed her goodbye. She was another victim I had tried to save along with various rescue personnel and I felt terrible about losing her. We exited the funeral home out into a cold drizzle and stood facing one another. I looked at both of them and said the two words I always said after such a sad event; "I'm sorry." The uncle immediately got angry, got in my face, and yelled, "Sorry, you don't know what the f--- sorry is, asshole." I was shocked! I had never been told this before at a body viewing. His wife immediately told him to shut up, apologized to me for his behavior, and they left with her driving. I kept my composure during the incident but he angered me, for I had a real good understanding of what sorry was all about. I lived it. I knew it was the alcohol talking not the man, but whenever I told someone I was sorry after that, this particular body identification surfaced in my mind. Saying "I'm sorry" became a much harder task for me than before, not because of the way I felt, I just didn't know what to expect after I said it. There seemed to be so many instances where people were stripped of their human spirit, and although I only acted as a first-hand witness and care provider, the nothingness left in the wake of human suffering took hold of me.

Between daily response calls and repetitive administrative duties I would mentally revisit past death scenes and autopsies, often pulling prior reports. My thoughts acting like the little white ball on a ping-pong table bouncing back and forth across the net of emergency services in a never-ending volley, each stroke of my recall paddle asking, "Are our roadways inferior?" "Did I miss something?" "Anything?" "Could I have done something different?" "Should I have?" "Could I have?" "Should I have?" Then as if missing the ball and having a point scored against me, there'd be a new volley of questions about a different case and I'd start the whole process over again.

I was brought up in a strict religious home. I believed in God but the more tragedy I saw the more I doubted he existed. I found myself questioning God's existence. If there was a God, out there, up there, somewhere, why in God's name was he allowing all of this madness to occur? I was taught God was good. God was merciful. Really? Well what about Townsend? Where was his mercy? Where was his goodness? I got angry with God. I got real angry with people who hurt other people. I even got angry with people who hurt themselves. On one occasion I thought about showing up at court and executing the killer standing trial. I had the means. I was one of only a few allowed to carry a concealed firearm inside the courtroom. This, however, would not solve anything. If I hurt another person I would become part of the problem for which I was desperately trying to find a solution. I could not solve the problem by lowering my intelligence to the level that had created the problem in the first place. My childhood teaching of God's Ten Commandments, specifically his sixth, "Thou Shall Not Kill," came flooding back into my mind. I was sworn to protect the lives and safety of others, even those charged with serious criminal offenses. Even killers. I was also trained to understand that the weapon I carried was issued to stop, not kill. There was no threat within the courtroom. There was no need to stop anyone. I was simply a referee in the game of life. My responsibility was to call the foul. A judge and jury would determine if my call was valid, and if it was, decide the penalty.

While questioning God's mercy I started to question my own. How much mercy is one person supposed to show toward evil? Suicides bothered me. I had to find a way to stop the senselessness of it all. Death was heavy on my mind. I was always an early bird, on the job by seven in the morning allowing time for interaction with the off-going midnight shift. I had always stayed connected to all three shifts; in before the midnight shift secured and out after the night shift came on duty in the afternoon. I found myself not wanting to go to work and would sit in the police station parking lot listening to the "oldies" on the radio until exactly eight o'clock on the button. In a sense I put myself on a time clock for a job that didn't have one. I dreaded being called on my police radio for emergency responses. I grew to hate the ring of my telephone at home, not knowing whether friend or foe was calling. By late 1989 I knew something was wrong with me but didn't know what.

Under my direction the police department sponsored a middle school boys and girls basketball program during the winter. The games were held on Saturdays, sponsored by the Townsend Police Athletic Association, and funded via private donations from local businesses. I attended games every Saturday morning at Hawthorne Brook Middle School and either coached or refereed games. The first sign of "my problem" came in the form of a youngster who walked past me wearing a Spaulding Memorial School tee shirt. The shirt was blue with a yellow logo, and had the name of the school printed on it in yellow as well. The exact same shirt Abigail Gustafson was wearing when we removed her body from the bathtub she was drowned in. When I saw the shirt the world around me went silent. I didn't hear anything in a gymnasium filled with kids. I just stood there frozen. I don't know for how long. I came out of my trance-like state by a child repeatedly pulling on my sleeve asking me a question. I knew something had happened to me but I didn't know what. Had I suffered some type of short-term stroke? I knew something wasn't right. About three weeks later I was alone with my one-year-old granddaughter when my world went silent again after seeing the OshKosh logo on the light green coveralls she was wearing. The exact color coveralls and logo five-year-old William Gustafson was wearing when we removed his body from the bathtub he was drowned in. As a result I went into another trance-like state and lost contact with my surroundings. This second event convinced me that I was in some type of medical trouble. I didn't know what was going on, but I knew something wasn't right in my head. I felt guilty for losing touch with my real world, even for just a moment, especially with the safety of my granddaughter in my hands. I was on call 24/7 everyday and was often called at home to respond to major incidents. I wasn't sleeping and would get up in the morning more tired than when I went to bed. I figured that I was perhaps suffering from fatigue due to a heavy work schedule. I sought help through my personal physician hoping to get back into a proper sleep cycle. As a result I started taking prescription medication to help me sleep. Shortly after that, I started taking medication to help me wake up. I found I couldn't function without them. I soon became addicted to Dexedrine and Halcion, taking a double dose of Halcion on my own at night to mellow me out and put me to sleep, or extra Dexedrine in the morning to get me moving. In a sense I was drinking heavy, except my bottle contained pills not booze. My need for increased doses of medication elevated my doctor's concern as to the amount of drugs I was taking. When I went to get refill prescriptions one afternoon he sat me down to talk about what was going on. After I honestly opened up to him about the many thoughts that were running rampantly through my mind he suggested I meet with a psychologist.

As result I met with Doctor Leo Polizoti in Worcester, Massachusetts. I soon found out what my problem was. I was suffering from severe post-traumatic stress disorder, or P.T.S.D. for short. You most likely have heard of this condition. I had. I often thought of it as an excuse used by some people to get disability medical retirement or work reduction benefits. I didn't think of it as a valid medical condition. I had served in the military. I was a career law enforcement officer. I had seen death and destruction in both arenas. In short, I was trained to kick ass and did whenever I had to. I was never taught to think for one minute that I could get beat up in return. Failure for me was not an option. Getting beat up was always a physical thing to me, which was probably why I never considered that my mind could be trampled. Not being able to physically see a real wound was perhaps the reason I didn't grasp what was going on. Bruising of the body was always a visual thing to me. Bodily injury in my world was clear-cut, usually consisting of skin discoloration, blood, or exposed bone and tissue. I had seen damaged brains in the field and autopsy room but viewed them simply as just another organ of the human body, especially in a damaged state. I never had reason to believe any other way, which perhaps explains why I never saw P.T.S.D. coming. In my medically-trained mind my brain wasn't damaged. Over time P.T.S.D. snuck up on me and knocked me right on my intellectual ass for almost the full count.

Working with Doctor Polizoti I learned that my trance episodes, which were ongoing, were "panic attacks" triggered by very vivid reminders of past horrific happenings, as were some of the nightmares I was having. I was connecting normal everyday images to past gruesome events. Not just clothing, but all kinds of things. Names. Dates. Locations. Someone simply asking, "Do you remember that case?" Of course I did. How could I forget it? How I wanted to forget it. Through medical intervention I found ways to avoid triggers and to suppress terrible thoughts. I started to read about post-traumatic stress and found it was a mental health condition triggered by a terrifying event. Anyone can develop the condition, regardless of age, after they experience an event that causes intense fear, helplessness, or horror. Just one horrific event can cause this condition, leaving those afflicted in a general state of existence characterized by hardship or mental suffering. If one event could cause the condition then Dr. Polizoti was correct with his diagnosis of me. I had witnessed many! I learned that post-traumatic stress disorder symptoms are generally grouped into three types: intrusive memories, avoidance, and increased anxiety & emotional arousal. Symptoms of intrusive memories may include flashbacks during waking moments or upsetting dreams of the traumatic event while asleep. Just what was happening to me! Avoidance symptoms, sometimes referred to as emotional numbing, include: trying to avoid thinking of the event, feeling emotionally numb, avoiding activities that once brought enjoyment, feeling hopeless about the future, trouble concentrating, memory problems and difficulty maintaining close relationships. I had some of that too! Symptoms of anxiety & emotional arousal may include: anger, irritability, shame, guilt, trouble sleeping, being easily frightened, and self-destructive behavior, such as excessive use of alcohol or drugs. With the exception of self-destructive behavior, I fit that category as well. As bad as it seemed I was happy to learn I had a "mental condition," not a "mental illness." Not that there would be any difference between the two if my condition became public knowledge. With a broken arm I'd be a hero, with a broken brain I'd be fired. Although I didn't feel good about keeping what was going on a secret, I felt better being able to understand "my condition." I had no problem visualizing injury to the body. I had worked with that for years. Now I could visualize my condition even though there was nothing to actually see.

Dr. Polizoti suggested I read about what others had lived through as a result of death and dying and recommended a book entitled "Man's Search for Meaning" by Viktor Frankl. Frankl had survived the horror of the Nazi concentration camps. His father, mother, brother, and his wife either died from starvation in the camp or were sent to the gas chamber. Except for his sister his entire family perished. During all of this he suffered from hunger, cold, brutality, and the fear of his own extermination at any moment. He had no possessions. He had lost everything except his mind, which under the circumstances was beyond amazing. In spite of the evil that surrounded him there was one thing his captors could not take from him; his freedom of thought. The freedom to determine his own attitude and spiritual well-being. He wrote his book to help others survive severe loss. The book proved to be of great benefit to me as it lessened my anger and frustration with what I had witnessed over the years. In his book, Frankl put forth the idea of thinking "this too shall pass" when faced with the sadness and grief that tragedy brings with it. I was taken by this particular passage. To survive day-to-day he had to live by this, however, I could sense in his writing that his "this too" did not pass. Nor would it. Ever. I mention this not as a criticism of his work but as an observation of just how hard post-traumatic stress can take hold of the individual mind. Surely everything will pass. Everything does, but passing isn't the problem. Forgetting, or better yet, erasing the past, that's the difficult part. How does someone eliminate the images of watching their entire family being put to death? How does someone forget something so horrible? I would suggest there is only one answer, "impossible."

During one of my first sessions with Doctor Polizoti I talked about how I felt I wasn't doing enough to protect my people. Wasn't doing all that I could to help my people. I felt like I was letting my people down. During the middle of what I was saying he stopped me and said, "I notice you use the term 'my people' repeatedly. Who are these people you call your people?" I replied, "The people of Townsend, you know, my people." "Look," he told me, "The people of Townsend are not your people. You do not have ownership of them. You sound like an Indian Chief overseeing his tribe; someone that has a last and final say on all matters brought before him. You don't possess that power. You are employed to enforce criminal law, and in your case, also provide the best emergency medical treatment possible. You have got to understand that there are some things you have no control over. Some matters, perhaps most, in which you do not have the final say. If you do all that you can do, all that you know how to do, and someone dies, that isn't your fault. Certainly I can understand how all these cases must impact you, but look at the other side. What chance would someone have had if you hadn't been there? At least you gave victims a chance. You gave them hope. How about people you have helped? You have to start looking at all the positive that you've achieved as well." He was stern in his voice and he wasn't telling me anything I didn't already know, but I needed someone to tell me in no uncertain terms where to draw the line, someone to put me in my proper place. He didn't care if I was Chief of Police. So what!

I was deeply concerned with the number of suicides I had intervened with or investigated. My youngest victim had been fourteen. I knew there was a suicide prevention hotline but questioned how many really gave that course of action much thought. As if someone so desperate was going to call and get a second opinion about taking their own life. I asked Doctor Polizoti if there was anything more I could do to reduce the number of suicides. He told me there were two things I could do to absolutely reduce the number. The first, I had to know in advance that someone was intending to take his or her own life. The second, I had to stay with that someone twenty-four hours a day, every day of the week; forever. I said, "That's impossible." "Well," said Dr. Polizoti, "I think you just answered your own question." With that comment my professional role with respect to suicide prevention became clearer yet difficult to accept. Our suicide discussion was over but the deliberate act of self-destruction would continue.

On my visits to Worcester I noticed an extremely large "LIQUOR" sign over a store just down the street from the doctor's office. The sign, lit day and night, was bright red in color and measured approximately eight feet in length with a height of about four feet. The letters were bold block style and extremely large. The sign fulfilled its intended purpose; it certainly captured my attention. I was being medically weaned off of my prescription medications and within a short period of time the liquor sign took on its own personality. There was no way I could avoid seeing it going to or coming from my appointments. The sign penetrated my spirit and called out to me, "Come on over Bill, have a drink, you'll feel better, I promise." I would look at it after my sessions and think, "You know you're right, one drink won't hurt." Although the temptations were many and great, I never stopped. I had seen so many lives destroyed because of excessive alcohol consumption. I knew that alcohol was a depressant as well as addictive. Although I knew this, Dr. Polizoti constantly reminded me. The last thing I needed was something that would take me deeper into despair. I couldn't afford to go further down inside my head. My emotions were suspended well below the surface of normal and I knew full well that I wouldn't survive at the bottom. I was also driving an unmarked police cruiser. I knew the rules relative to drunk driving. If I was employed to enforce them, then I was also required to abide by them. So I can't say I don't know why I didn't stop and buy "a bottle" because I knew. Acknowledging right from wrong, as hard as it was, as basic as it seems, proved to be a turning point for me. Something that was taught to me at an early age proved to be the foundation for making the right decision in this instance. As a police officer I had witnessed countless consequences of bad decisions made by people who could have, and often should have, made better ones. I had no excuse. I wanted to get better. I don't know who owned the liquor store but I thank them for hanging that brightly lit sign. For as lost as I was with the amount of death and destruction being re-run inside my head, that sign brightened my life, and although I didn't follow the path it wanted me to take, it sure did point me in the right direction; it showed me the way not to go.

Some of my therapeutic sessions seemed to last forever but only took less than an hour. I would visually encounter other patients going to or coming from my appointments and wondered what brought them to the same place I was visiting. What brought them so far down? We never spoke. Didn't have to. I always made it a point to make eye contact with these people. Some never looked up at me and I could feel their despair just by their failure to acknowledge my presence. Was their world so dark they didn't even see me? Were their failures to acknowledge my presence deliberate acts of omission, or were they really that lost? As strange as it seems, this failure of the other person to acknowledge me by making simple eye contact made me realize that maybe I wasn't as close to the bottom of my psychological pit as I had assumed. Maybe I had reached my lowest point and wouldn't go any deeper. Had I leveled off? Maybe, just maybe, I was starting to climb out of my hole. The few people that did make eye contact did simply that. No facial expressions, no words spoken, just quick slanted looks. Nothing more. Nothing meant. I could sense with these people, even at their slightly higher level of "wellness," they weren't too far from the bottom either. I found comfort along the street or in the parking garage where an occasional encounter would include solid eye-to-eye contact with other people, followed by facial expressions, and on some occasions, words of greeting. How refreshing to get out into this "well" world. I looked forward to these "outer encounters," and over time I grew to understand, just by simple eye movements, or the lack thereof, just how desperate some people were. I found it interesting that my sessions extended beyond the confines of the doctor's office and out onto the street. For as bad as it got for me I was always able to make eye contact with other people, always able to say hello. I wasn't trying to openly hide what was going on inside my head, just trying to live with it without others knowing.

During some of my sessions I talked to Dr. Polizoti about quitting my job. I was deep in debt with a mortgaged home and other monthly payments. What could I change to? The work I knew best was law enforcement and I was good at what I did. Changing to another line of work wasn't a sound option in my mind, nor was keeping my profession and working in another community an option either. All this would do was relocate my problem. One of the major issues I faced were the continuous triggers that living and working in my community presented. Once an idyllic home of boyhood adventures, my hometown had become a place of troubled times. Every street had reminders, which I would pass by day after day. My marriage had ended a few years earlier and I was on my own to make any changes I felt would help me. As such, I bought a home high on a hill overlooking a valley ten miles from Townsend. This move proved to be my lifesaver. I would pass an old farmhouse with a mountain set behind it on my way home from work each day. This one spot became the "on and off" switch for my workday. I knew I could be called at home at any hour, but when I passed this special location, my workday and whatever it contained got shut off as best it could. From continued consultation my life didn't take a turn at the fork in the road, instead I went both ways. I followed the low road of my profession, did what I was required to do, and the high road of my personal life, and did what made me feel good. I sought and found the good along both roads, and did whatever I could to shut off anything bad that came my way. I learned that my survival in a job that produced so many sad conclusions hinged on my ability to focus equally on events that brought happiness with them. If not absolute joy every time, at least some degree of contentment or interest. Something that gave me the personal satisfaction of knowing I made a difference to some extent or left me feeling good about what some other person might be doing.

After twelve months of treatment and slowly decreasing dosage, I stopped taking prescription medications. I found that whenever a tragic memory surfaced I had the power to submerge it with a happier one. Part of my inner healing came from ideas I found in books I read about death and dying. One thing that stuck with me was to do good for others without the expectation of a thank you. As such I started to visit nursing homes after work in uniform to either play cards or just sit and talk with elderly people. Many were lonely and for the most part "Father Time" was their only, yet constant visitor. From there I visited young people in rehabilitation units, some I knew because I was there when they injured their bodies. I became important to a special group of people, and they became just as important to me. They didn't know it, but they gave me more than they realized, for when I lifted their spirits up, so did they raise mine. Love comes in many forms. A simple "Hello, how are you doing?" to someone stuck in a room at an elderly nursing home translates into "I care about you," and for those who have no one, "I love you." I found I had to work at being happy and in the process realized it was such an easy task. Casual observations of people going about their daily routines became an important part of my existence. For me it was way to keep my mind in an active state rather than a passive one. I sought out the good in people and sought to do good for people. Not that I hadn't before, but when you experience the very worst in people, especially evil beings, seeking out the good in people takes on far greater meaning. I started to exercise and often walked three miles a day. I would get out of my cruiser and walk into the woods to look around and see how the seasons were affecting the environment. Had anything changed in a particular area since my last visit? Fallen limbs, leaves, and pine needles coupled with snow arrival or departure dates can tell a story of their own to a criminal investigator. Mother Nature has a way of telling the truth and I would make notes dating existing conditions. I became addicted to a new drug called "fresh air," and would fill my lungs and brain with it whenever I could. My need for prescription medications ceased to exist. I ended my sessions with Dr. Polizoti in the fall of 1991. I was back on track. I didn't know exactly where my professional train was headed or what might be waiting around the bend, but at least I had my hand on the throttle. I was back in control. I wasn't a train wreck waiting to happen anymore.

# CHAPTER 15

## SAFETY FIRST
### SPRING 1992

Each year during the early weeks of June I had the pleasure of going to visit students in grades K-4 at Spaulding Memorial School to speak with them about safety. I had a workshop in my cellar and constructed a small wooden school bus, convertible car, and a road for these two vehicles to roll down. At the end of the road, which was about four feet long with raised edges, I attached a red wall for the vehicles to crash into. I also made a variety of little wooden people that were round in shape with smaller round heads with flat bottoms that fit into round holes drilled into the vehicles, which were viewed as seats or standing positions. These little people came in assorted colors of hair, clothing, and skin. The bus these animated students traveled on had a hole for the driver, a series of two holes for seats on both sides for students, and a hole in the middle in the back for the "kid" that didn't sit down but should have.

I would talk to students about the importance of sitting in their seats, the dangers of standing, while reminding everyone "we always keep our hands to ourselves." I would use the little wooden people and bus to demonstrate what happens to the "kid" that stands in the back when the bus stopped unexpectedly. All the seat holes were drilled deeper than the one for the "standing kid" so when the bus hit the wall the "standing kid" soon became the "flying kid" while all the others remained "seated." I would capitalize on the vast imaginations of my young audience and start the bus safety talk with my little wooden people talking to each other. I'd point them toward one another and they'd say, "Hi, how ya doing?" "Did you do your homework?" "Yeah, did you?" All the voices would be mine of course but the kids bought right into my presentation because they were looking at the little wooden figures and not my lips. As planned there would be the wooden kid in the back of the bus that was standing after he was told by the driver to sit in a seat. I would then hold the road up about a foot high opposite the crash wall and remind the group what was about to happen to the kid that was standing when the bus hit the wall, and that perhaps we shouldn't let the bus crash. Of course this brought about a tremendous amount of cheering to "Do it, do it, do it!" I would give in to the crowd as planned and roll the bus down the road where it would hit the wall, and the "standing kid" would go "flying." This crash dynamic would startle my young audience at first, and then they would erupt in laughter. I pointed out that we could laugh when the people weren't real, but how tragic the accident would have been if the little person that went "flying" was one of their friends, or even worse, "you!"

I would select four "helpers" to help me out in the third and fourth grades, and found there was always an abundance of willing participants. The first student would play the role of emergency telecommunications operator, and we'd review how to dial "911" and what to say. The three others would be "on-scene" emergency people: police officer, rescue firefighter, and emergency medical technician. Each would play their role accordingly. I had two wooden families, the "Red" family and the "Blue," that rode in the convertible that had round holes drilled into it for seats, two in the front and two in the back. The convertible had imaginary seat belts in the bottom of the "seats" that was one side Velcro. There were four members in each family, mother, father, daughter, son, and they were painted one color only to represent their family name. The Red family, Mr. Red, Mrs. Red, Roberta Red, and Ryan Red had Velcro on their bottoms. When placed inside the little vehicle these simulated seat belts would keep them in their seats when the convertible crashed into the wall. The Blue family of course didn't wear their seat belts; they didn't have any Velcro on their bottoms. There was Mr. Blue, Mrs. Blue, Betty

Blue, and their son. I would always ask if anyone knew the son's name, which would set the little minds in my audience into motion. Every now and then someone would know his name; "Little Boy Blue!" I would hesitate before sending the Blue family to their doom, and ask the school children, "Do you think we should do this?" Of course the crowd would shout out "Do it, do it, do it!" I would raise the roadway sending the Blue family down the highway where they would hit the wall sending them flying off in all different directions. This proved to be the main event, the one thing that really got my little crowd's attention, causing great excitement to fill the air. Then my little police officer, rescue firefighter, and emergency medical technician "helpers" would do their jobs sending the Blue family off to the imaginary hospital. We would then talk about the importance of wearing seat belts, and although our imaginary crash was funny, together we learned a real life crash without seat belts was quite serious.

My presentations would last for about forty-five minutes. There were many words of advice. "Don't go swimming alone, wear your seat belt, don't talk to strangers, wear your bike helmet, sit in your seat, and keep your hands to yourself." I shortened my presentation for kindergarten classes, and squeezed everything into about twenty minutes to accommodate an audience with short attention spans. I always ended my talk by asking if there were any questions. Four-year-olds are a tremendous amount of fun to work with. I never knew what to expect or what I'd hear. Sometimes instead of questions I would get comments like, "My uncle is in jail," or, "Our dog got hit by a car." Over time I felt I had heard it all until I came up against the toughest group of four-year-olds I had ever encountered. I had just completed my twenty-minute thrill-packed safety presentation before this special kindergarten class of fifteen wide-eyed boys and girls. While they sat in a semi-circle I asked the group if anyone had any questions. I had been introduced as "Chief May" so one girl raised her hand and asked if I lived in a house or a teepee. Another wanted to know if Mr. May, the school principal, was my father. Although we shared the same last name we were not related but were somewhat close in age. Although the answer was "No," the question coupled with the answer was a compliment of sorts as it made me feel younger. As I stood basking in my newfound youth the arm of a four-year-old boy shot up. I asked him his name to which he forcefully responded, "Jonathan." Before I could ask what his question was he proceeded to speak. He told me I had "Forgotten to mention the two most unsafe things in North America." I was immediately impressed because he was only four years old and knew where North America was. There were some students in high school that had trouble finding North America on a global map. Plus he was correcting me, the Chief of Police, the "safety expert" extraordinaire. I looked at the teacher in the back of the room and she looked back at me. We looked at each other with that "What the heck?" expression on our faces, not knowing what was coming next. Jonathan continued along with his safety presentation without stopping. "The first thing, Chief May, is the black widow spider, the female one. You can tell if it's a female because it will have a yellow belly with a pink dot. The second is the diamond back rattlesnake." While pointing to the back of his neck he continued, "You can tell if it's a diamond back rattler because it will have diamond marks on the back of its neck. If you get bitten or stung by either one of these you could get very sick or --- DIE!" The room fell silent. His classmate's eyes seemed to bulge out of their little heads. He came right out with it. The worst safety word of all; "DIE!"

Talk about getting everyone's attention. I was stunned. My stuff about keeping our hands to ourselves, wearing our bike helmets, not talking to strangers, and sitting in our seats was commonplace compared to Jonathan's "bite and die" extravaganza.

# AFTERMATH:

After this class I decided to include black widow spiders and diamond back rattlesnakes in all my future kindergarten safety presentations. I also did away with accepting any questions from young audiences as well. I figured I'd be better off heading them off at the "Nothing Said Pass" rather than get shot up again in another verbal ambush.

Honesty was what made this little vignette amusing. I had the opportunity to experience many. I found throughout my career that being morally upright ran strong among children. When a bad situation presented itself and I needed to know the truth, and there was a child present, I'd ask the child. A sad commentary about the grown up world I guess, but true.

# CHAPTER 16

# OLYMPIC GOLD
## SUMMER 1992

The opening ceremony of the 1992 Barcelona Summer Olympics has been heralded as one of the most magnificent in sporting memory! Dancers clad all in white danced Catalonia's traditional circular Sardana dance thus echoing the Olympic rings, Jose Carreras and Monserrat Caballé performed Freddie Mercury's sensational "Barcelona" anthem (given added poignancy by the recent death of the Queen musical group front man), and Paralympic archer Antonio Rebollo lit the Olympic flame by dramatically shooting a fire-lit arrow over the heads of the crowd into the Olympic cauldron. The 1992 Games were underway!

Just a few weeks before all of this happened, a young female gymnast named Shannon Miller of the United States captivated the imagination of many young women around the world. Shannon was poised to win the gold medal in the balance beam competition at the summer games, as well as other medals in gymnastics. Shannon was an inspiration, especially to young girls around the world who wanted to be a champion just like she was. She ignited the dream of becoming a gold medalist in young women just like Antonio Rebollo had fired up the flame of the Olympic cauldron.

I lived about ten miles from the Townsend Police Station and would travel one of two basic routes going to and from work. I would often vary my route of travel taking various side roads to see what was going on in different sections of town. Sometimes I would conduct a "loop around" which would take me out of Townsend and then place me back in town on a different road. This allowed me to view homes and properties on the outer fringes. I drove a fully equipped unmarked Ford Crown Victoria police cruiser. Although it looked like an ordinary vehicle, there were emergency blue lights hidden inside the front grille section as well as on the upper platform behind the rear seat. The trunk was equipped with various pieces of emergency equipment; throw rope, fire extinguisher, pry bar, first aid kit, oxygen, blanket, and a semi-automatic rifle. I carried an orange emergency medical "grab and go" jump kit that rode with me on the front passenger seat, which provided for quick and immediate access. This bag contained the basic tools for rapid response and treatment. Airways of various sizes, scissors capable of cutting through seat belts, bandages of various types, and an assortment of other materials including a stethoscope and blood pressure measuring device known in the business as a "blood cuff." I also had vehicle and portable two-way radio contact with my communications center. In short, I had the tools, training, and backup assistance needed to handle anything out of the ordinary that came my way, especially emergencies.

On June 4th I had worked until well after midnight and didn't go into work until two o'clock the following day. I decided to conduct a routine patrol before tackling the paperwork that awaited me at my desk. Patrols came easy for me compared to the paperwork, which I always had to pump myself up for. Conducting a patrol was a good way to ease my way back into the daily grind of driving a desk. I drove to West Townsend, went south on West Elm Street, and then east onto Bayberry Hill Road. As I came around a corner in the road I saw four young girls who were screaming hysterically. They appeared to be about twelve years old or so. One girl was holding the front of her lower face and I could clearly see blood streaming out from the area of her mouth, between her fingers, and down her arms. I immediately radioed my control center for emergency medical and police backup assistance before getting out of my police cruiser. I grabbed my emergency medical jump kit and ran directly to the girl who was bleeding. She had a severe laceration that extended through her upper lip and continued upward along one side of her face parallel to her nose. Her wound first appeared to be about three inches in length. I knew I had to stop the bleeding, maintain an open airway, and prevent her from going into shock as best I could. I sat her down on the front passenger seat in my cruiser. I wanted to place her on her back and elevate her feet to slow the shock process down, but her bleeding was so severe I feared she would asphyxiate on her own blood. Putting her in a flat position would only cause a greater amount of blood to flow to her head. In most cases getting the most blood possible to the brain is a good thing. This was one of those exceptions.

I scanned the area looking for some type of wreckage and didn't see any. These girls were too young to drive, but I felt there could have been an accident and the vehicle was perhaps out of my line of sight. Maybe there were other injured people I couldn't see. For the first few seconds I couldn't determine how this girl got hurt so badly. Through the three panicked voices of her friends I learned my victim's name was Alyssa. I started calling her by her name right away to form a "we know each other" bond. I soon found out that the girls had been practicing Olympic "balance beam" techniques on the metal guardrail that ran alongside the roadway. The girl I was tending to had slipped and fallen from the guardrail and hit the upright I-beam that held the guardrail in place. She clipped the corner of it with her mouth and suffered a traumatic extraction of her left upper front middle tooth along with a serious jagged three-inch incision to her face. I applied direct pressure to my young victim's open wound by holding gauze pads in place. Bleeding as a result of a wound to the head is difficult to stop. This wound was further compounded by the fact that she was lacerated inside her mouth as well. She presented two radical incisions, basically one on top of the other. She needed to be sewn back together. She suffered from excessive blood loss, a condition that had to be immediately addressed. She was going into shock. She needed emergency room care and she needed it quick!

In an effort to control the panic around me I put the other three girls to work. This calmed them down as well as helped me accomplish some things I couldn't do while trying to stabilize my victim. I had one girl assist me by passing me material I needed from my jump kit. I told the other two girls to cross over the street to where my victim had fallen to see if they could locate the missing tooth. I was astonished when they came running back within a minute with tooth in hand. I had the first girl hold the tooth on a sterile gauze pad and told the same two girls that found the tooth to go to Marge Kumpu's house, which was just down the road, and tell her that Chief May needed a cup of milk right away for an emergency. I felt relieved when they quickly came back with Marge and a cup of milk. I dropped the extracted tooth into the protein rich milk to preserve any tissue still attached. I kept reminding my victim that she was in good hands, that I was trained in emergency medicine, and everything would work out fine. She was semi-conscious, and presented no visible indication of brain injury. She was doing as best possible for the bad situation she was in. The backup units arrived, emergency medical technicians took over, and my victim was rushed away by ambulance. I requested my communications center contact the girl's parents so they could go to the hospital to give their consent for further medical treatment of their daughter. I then drove the other three girls to their homes.

I had heard through inner channels that Alyssa was doing very well. The following week I received a thank you note in the mail from her mother. Over time in the police profession you lose track of people. Jumping from one event to the next leaves little time, if any, to follow up on what happened in the past. Every day is different. Hours of calm can be interrupted by moments of complete chaos that must be brought under immediate control. That's what Alyssa and I shared. Just when you think you've seen it all something new happens to make you realize you hadn't. Often during these fast-paced moments faces become blurred, especially the injured ones. As time went by, Alyssa became a faded happy memory.

# AFTERMATH:

A little over three years had passed since the tooth incident. I was sitting at a table in Townsend Pizza eating my lunch in October 1995 when two young ladies walked in. They strolled to the counter behind my back and I heard them place their order for lunch. I didn't think much of it until I felt a tap on my shoulder and heard, "Hello Chief May. Do you remember me?" I stood up and faced the young woman and said "Hello," but I couldn't put a name to her face. She looked familiar but having dealt with so many people under so many different and often difficult circumstances I couldn't place her face to a definitive event. So I said, "I kind of remember you but I'm sorry, I can't put a name to your face." She responded with "Well that's understandable Chief May because the last time you saw me up close my face was covered with blood. I'm Alyssa, the girl that lost her tooth on the guardrail." I couldn't believe my eyes. There was no sign of the serious injury she had suffered. She then pulled her upper lip up to show me her tooth and said, "See my tooth? That's my real tooth. The one you put in the cup of milk. They implanted it at the hospital and it's as if it never came out of my mouth. See my face? I had plastic surgery and you'd never even know I got cut there either." I said, "Alyssa I'm so happy for you. You look absolutely beautiful." With that she gave me a big hug and said, "Thank you so much for being there for me." "Well," I said, "I'm just happy everything worked out as well as it did." We just stood there for a moment with our eyes welling up. I finished my lunch, exchanged parting comments, and walked to my police cruiser. I had just experienced one of those "feel good" moments; one that doesn't come in a paycheck no matter how much money you make.

Shannon Miller, suffering from a sport related injury, came in second and won the silver medal in the balance beam competition in Barcelona in 1992. She went on to win the gold at the Olympic games in 1996. Alyssa Transue fully recovered from her injuries with the help of a real good medical team. She is now 32 years old, engaged to be married, and has a gold medal smile. Each of these women in there own individual way represented the strength sometimes required to overcome adversity. Alyssa recently told me that she clearly recalls seeing me running toward her on that day so long ago, wondering, "Where did he come from so fast?" She was, after all, out in the woods along a backcountry road in serious need of medical help. I often wonder too. What prompted me to patrol that road, on that day, at the precise moment I was needed? I'll never know the answer to that question. The ability for me to succeed in this instance was a direct result of my training, but deep down inside I feel a much higher power put me on that road.

# CHAPTER 17

# THE WALL
## SPRING 1994

One thing I truly enjoyed was working outside on my property. My home sat atop a high hill overlooking a large valley and the mountains to the north. I looked forward to going home after work for it provided me not only the solace needed to survive unwanted memories of past tragic events, but the relief needed to tolerate the day-to-day intolerance that came with the job as well. The hundreds of petty issues, sometimes linked to politics, that seemed to burn tremendous amounts of good energy in wasteful ways. Working outside recharged my body battery, supplied fresh air to my brain, and conditioned me for my tomorrows, whether they proved trivial or traumatic. I was on-call while off duty every day of the year and there was a written order of when I was to be called. Murder, suicide, rape, serious accident, and armed robbery topped the many reasons on the list, right down to "when uncertain about what to do." I ran a tight ship and the people that worked with me knew it. I was very fortunate. I worked with the very best, and together we achieved the extraordinary.

There was a large field behind my home with rocks and small boulders strewn about, left where they came to rest years ago during the Ice Age. To put this material to good use, as well as clean up the field, I decided to build a stonewall along the roadway in front of my property. Once completed, the freestanding wall would measure two hundred fifty feet long with a height and width of three feet. I purchased a used thirty-five horsepower tractor and gathered the necessary tools needed to do stonework: pry bars, chains, hammers, chisels, and gloves. This was to be a long-term project to add value to my property, but more importantly add strength to my mind and body. I was ready for the challenge.

After reading a couple of articles about how to construct stonewalls I set about the task. I soon found out that rocks don't enjoy being moved from their original resting place, and put up resistance directly proportional their size. Some put up a great fight simply because of their shape. Rocks aren't readily moved. They must be pried from their location. After a while I found myself talking to rocks as if they were human. "Come on you little stinker, I haven't got all day," was often my thought. On some occasions I would replace "stinker" in my thought process and use the "s---" word instead. Every now and then I would painfully pinch my finger between two rocks but for some reason, perhaps because I had no one to answer to, the thought of yelling "prunes" never crossed my mind. At times I would actually verbalize my frustration and speak out loud to the rocks as if they could actually understand my frustration. Rocks are very much like owning a pet dog. Dogs don't mean to cause you grief, but when they do they just look at you, and wag their tail. Rocks take it to a lower level. They don't have tails to wag so they just sit and look at you.

No sooner had I found out how hard rocks were to move, I found out they were even harder to put in place. The first one, the one on the bottom, is not as challenging as those that rise above; those middle stones that must fit into a specific space and interlock. I developed names for the rocks: bottom rock, wedge rock, connecting rock, top rock, and so on. I became obsessed with rocks and took particular notice of them on my drives around town, or when going to or coming home from work. Rocks took on certain personas. Some I would see on a daily basis and I could imagine how the "better ones" would work well into my project. I wanted to start an "Adopt A Rock" program and bring those special ones home, but these little babies were more like one hundred pounds, well above the average seven-pound birth weight. Realizing the general population would think I was off my rocker advocating such a far out rock-friendly idea coupled with the fact that most were too heavy, I scrapped the "Adopt A Rock" idea before it materialized.

By the summer of 1994 I was really rocking without any music. I had rocks all over my front yard, and although I didn't have names for each one of them, I knew each one by size and shape. By late summer I had completed about one hundred feet of my stone masterpiece. Working alongside the roadway provided me with an opportunity to talk with people passing by. Many complimented me on the work I was doing and I was pleased with the progress I was making. I had my back to the roadway one afternoon when I heard a vehicle slow down and stop. I turned just in time to see that it was a pickup truck and that it was backing up on the opposite side of the street in my direction. The truck went past me in reverse, stopped again, and then came back in my direction, pulling up alongside me on my side of the road, whereupon the operator shut the engine off. The truck, which was dirty and had a few dents, appeared to be the typical construction worker's home away from home. Shovels, hoes, and rakes were stacked just after the cab, and there was a variety of assorted items in the bed: hardhats, grub hoes, wheelbarrows, loose assorted hand tools, sections of garden hose, and a portable air compressor to mention a few.

The truck was a double cab unit and there were four men sitting in it: two in the front and two in the back. All four appeared to be dirty from a hard day of work. I made a quick face check on each one of them and determined no one looked familiar to me, so I doubted I was in for any type of confrontation based upon a past police experience. Each man was holding a twenty-four ounce can of beer in one hand and a lit cigarette in the other. The windows were down in the truck and we exchanged the typical "How ya doing?" greeting often used by strangers who want to engage in conversation with an unknown other. The operator, who I sensed was the leader of the pack, took a swig of beer and said, "Nice 'f---ing' wall you got there," after which he exhaled a long slow puff from his cigarette. I smiled, thanked him for his "over the top" compliment, and judging by the trail of his cigarette smoke, was pleased to see that I was standing upwind from where he was sitting. I figured this guy was quite familiar with the difficult work I was doing and truly understood how labor-intensive masonry work was. He continued with his "f---ing" laced praise and I thanked him again for his compliments. Then he asked, "How 'f---ing' long have you been working on it?" I told him I had been at it for about five months. I sensed I should have responded with "Five 'f---ing' months" which would have brought my reply down to his level and bonded us in a sick sort of way, but stuck to the higher ground instead. The other three guys in the truck continued to drink their beer and smoke their cigarettes. They just listened to what the driver had to say, validating my initial opinion that he was the man in charge. He looked at the wall again and then asked me, "Are you a 'f---ing' mason or something?" "No I'm not a mason," I said, "I'm just doing this as a hobby." I also wanted to tell him I wasn't a "something" either but I had a hard time trying to figure out what a something actually was, so I let that part of his question slide. "A 'f---ing' hobby," he replied, "You've got to be out of your "f---ing' mind." "Not really," I countered, "I really enjoy just being outside in the fresh air and working with the stones." He looked at me for a moment and then asked, "Do you work in 'f---ing' town here?" "No," I said, sensing our conversation was starting to head downhill. "I work in Townsend, about ten miles from here," I continued. I knew what was coming next. I knew our conversation was about to be terminated. Then came his next question, the coup de grace. "What the 'f---' do you do in Townsend?" "I'm the Chief of Police there," I told him. With that he started the truck up, put it in gear, and abruptly drove off. Never said, "Nice to 'f---ing' meet ya", or "Good 'f---ing' luck on that wall." Nothing. Didn't say another word, which in my mind displayed a total lack of hospitality on his part.

# AFTERMATH:

I completed the wall in the fall of 1995. From the work I did I grew to appreciate the many stone walls I often saw running along roadways, across fields, and through woods in my native New England. They were constructed back before the age of the tractor, by men using horse-drawn stone sleds and crowbars. Each stone wall a lasting tribute to the hard labor of a forgotten past. I never saw the pickup truck again. I surmise that friendship wasn't meant to be. Never meant to endure over time, like stone walls do.

# CHAPTER 18

# TIMOTHY REGAN

## SPRING 1996

I first met Timothy Regan in 1992 during one of my kindergarten "keep your hands to yourself – wear your bike helmet" safety talks at Spaulding Memorial School. One of my older style presentations that didn't include snakes or spiders, and allowed children to ask or say anything they wanted to at the conclusion of my presentation. Tim had a smile that ran from ear to ear and eyes that lit up as if they were backlit by 200-watt bulbs. He was by all accounts one happy kid. Tim didn't walk into my safety class and sit on the gymnasium floor like his classmates, however; Tim wheeled himself into the gym seated in an electrically motorized scooter. He also had lower leg braces to stabilize his upper body when in the standing position, and his hands didn't flex as easily as his classmates. Tim had been born with cerebral palsy, a life-long condition, but he didn't stand out from the crowd for visibly obvious reasons. What made this boy exceptional was his zest for life. In spite of the difficulties he faced, he liked to laugh and went about his daily routine with a smile upon his face.

As the years passed by we became good friends. I would see him upon occasion, and at my request, he rode beside me in my police car one year while leading the Memorial Day parade. At age nine Tim wanted a three-wheel bike that he could power by either foot pedals or moving the handlebars back and forth. Something he could do on his own without the need of a battery pack. Power could be applied to the trike by using either method or the combination of both. Tim's parents, Nancy and Bill Regan, were pushing the idea as well, for in addition to being a fun thing to do, the trike also provided the physical exercise Tim required. He was constantly in physical therapy and the trike would give him a break from that routine and provide him with a happier form of rehabilitation. A company in Texas under the brand name Rock and Roll Cycles manufactured the trike, and each one was custom fit to the individual needs of the person intending to use it. In conjunction with the tricycle there was a "Shine-A-Light" safety program where the money required for purchasing the trike could be raised by selling safety lights. The lights sold for ten dollars each and could be attached to a bicycle or clothing for use at night. Tim would have to sell two hundred lights in order to receive his tricycle at no cost to him.

I got word about Tim's desire to get a tricycle and how he wanted to "buy" a Rock and Roll unit on his own. I had many people who worked with me on a day-to-day basis, including Kate Walsh, editor of the "Townsend Times," the local newspaper. I contacted Kate and ran the idea by her about holding a news conference at the police station to announce Tim's intentions. Always willing to help, Kate told me she would have a reporter and photographer attending. I circulated a memo outlining the event within the various emergency services departments and everyone jumped onboard the Tim Regan Rock and Roll Express. On an April afternoon Tim came to the police station at four o'clock to conduct his press conference. Before going into the meeting he stopped by my office. After looking around, he said, "Your office sure is messy." Talk about biting the hand that feeds you! So I joked back about how I bet his room wasn't much better. Thus the tone of the day was set. Not unusual for a boy who really enjoyed a good joke.

We went downstairs to the press conference and the room was filled with news people and emergency service workers. Tim was the star of the show with his ever-constant smile and quick wit. The plan was to sell the lights every Saturday, week after week, starting on May 4th from 7:30AM to 1PM at Cliff's Cafe in the center of town, until Tim sold enough lights to buy his tricycle. During the announcement I asked Tim if he could get up that early on Saturday to which he replied, "You got to be kidding me." 'Hey," I said, "It's just like getting up for school." The comments continued, Tim and I playing verbal "Got ya!" back and forth, until the conference ended.

The next day Tim's picture, along with the story of his mission, appeared on the front page of the weekly newspaper. I was sitting at my desk reading the article when my telephone rang. The caller identified himself as Michael McCauliff from Fitchburg, Massachusetts. He told me he had read the article in the paper and wanted to purchase the tricycle for Tim. He told me he had contacted the company in Texas that manufactured the tricycle and he could have one air freighted to Massachusetts in time for Tim's "Shine-A-Light-Buy-A-Trike" event on Saturday. All he needed to know was the color and options Tim wanted, along with the boy's height, weight, and particular needs. Since the special tricycle we were discussing was expensive I asked Michael if he knew the amount of money we were talking about. He let me know he did, including the cost of flying the bike in for Saturday, and figured he'd be spending in the area of sixteen hundred dollars. Further, he wanted the tricycle to be a surprise. I told Michael I knew Tim wanted a blue tricycle but felt it best that he speak with Tim's parents about weight, height, and specific needs, and gave him the Regan's telephone number. The next day Michael called me back to tell me he would be delivering the tricycle as planned on Saturday, probably around noon or so, now just five days away! Talk about the unbelievable!

On Friday evening, the night before Tim's first big sales event, Mike McCauliff, his brother Timothy, and friends Norman Pare and Richard Hanley drove to Logan International Airport in Boston, picked up the tricycle, and then drove back to Fitchburg spending most of the night assembling it. In the morning they put the finishing touches on the tricycle and made it ready for delivery. I didn't know it at the time but these four young men put in equal amounts of time, money, and effort to make the "tricycle surprise" happen.

On Saturday morning at 7:30 I met Tim at Cliff's Cafe as planned and we set up a sales table right next to the main entrance. As usual

Tim was all smiles and full of enthusiasm. People started to arrive slowly at first and then more frequently as the morning moved on. One light was sold and then another, Tim meeting the people and they him. One fellow stopped, shook Tim's hand, told Tim he admired him, put one hundred bucks on the table and walked away with ten lights. Sales were going really well as the noon hour approached. At exactly twelve o'clock a yellow El Camino sport utility pickup pulled up across the street from the cafe with a covered bundle in the back. A stranger got out and walked over to Tim, took his hand and said, "I have something for you." I stopped the traffic so this man and Tim could safely cross the street. The man, surrounded by his three companions, also unknown to the crowd, took Tim over to the El Camino. He lifted the tarp as Tim watched. Beneath was the blue Columbia tricycle Tim had hoped to earn by June. With that, this stranger known to me as Mike McCauliff said, "This is for you." At first Tim couldn't believe his eyes, which had instantly grown to silver dollar size. Tim had used a "loaner" tricycle the year before and his first reaction was the new tricycle he was looking at was another "loaner." Mike explained to Tim that the tricycle he was looking at was a gift that he could keep and take home. Tim was beyond happy and gave the tricycle a trial run right there on Main Street. There wasn't a dry eye in the crowd.

Within four hours Tim had sold just over one hundred forty lights. Sales no longer needed for the goal he had set. In return Tim gave his sales to Jason Dold, age 11, who had a similar need and wanted a tricycle of his own, except red in color. Ironically Jason had sold the number of lights required for his tricycle but gave his sales to Adam Cale of Macomb, Illinois as a Christmas present. Adam was only six years old, needed a tricycle as well, but had trouble selling the lights. Just like in the movies, Mike McCauliff and his band of merry men rode off into the sunset.

# AFTERMATH:

Tim Regan graduated from high school in 2005. Rather than go right off to college he decided to take a cross-country trip in 2006 with two of his buddies in Tim's Ford Escape. Appropriately named, the vehicle provided the three of them with a means of breaking out of small town America. They had a blast! The trip took seven weeks to complete. Tim then started college but left after his second year. He volunteered to work at the Texas Lions Camp in Kerrville, Texas, a nonprofit camp for children with physical disabilities, as well as those with cancer, burns, diabetes, and Down's syndrome. He lasted one summer there because he found the Texas heat was too extreme. He then went to work as a volunteer camp counselor at Victory Junction, a kid's summer camp in Randleman, North Carolina. Victory Junction is located on 84 acres donated by Richard Petty, of NASCAR fame, and his wife Lynda. They are also actively involved in the overall operation of the facility that accommodates children with 24 chronic medical conditions and serious illnesses: autism, cancer, craniofacial anomalies, diabetes, hemophilia, sickle cell, and spina bifida to mention a few. Thirty hospitals have partnered with Victory Junction to deliver exceptional care to campers with a variety of medical needs. There is a different week for every illness, which provides for the best possible medical staffing to be on hand. Tim told me he enjoys working with the kids regardless of their setbacks, but looks forward to cerebral palsy week most of all because he fully understands what those kids are up against. He also said, "I feel extremely lucky with what I got," referring to his cerebral palsy. Those were his exact words. As long as I have known Tim he has never asked, "Why me?" He faces his battle against cerebral palsy every day with a tremendous determination underneath his smile. He walks much better than he did as a child and has better use of his hands, yet the damage that cerebral palsy did to his body is still visible. He can do most of what his friends do except he tires much faster than they do. Years of physical therapy, including riding many miles on his special tricycle have truly helped him. In 2009 Tim lost his longtime girlfriend Kerry, who passed away as a result of cerebral palsy and spina bifida complications. Something he has learned to accept and live with, and expresses this loss in her terms more than his own. He is presently attending North Carolina State University and is scheduled to graduate in 2013 with a degree in computer science. His goal is to go back to counsel kids at Victory Junction. Based on his past performance he'll be there for the 2013 summer season.

There is an expression these days, "It is what it is." I have never liked this saying for it speaks to the commonplace, a general acceptance of the world around us absent the possibility of change for the better. A close relative of the failure phrase, "Whatever happens, happens." Tim, Jason, Kate Walsh, the people who stopped to purchase lights, and the four strangers who came to Townsend bearing a special gift speak to a much different philosophy, a far greater standard; "It is what you make it!" Each one in their own way saw a real need and did something to change things for the better. Each in their own way chose to make a difference and it all started because a nine-year-old boy had a goal. Not a dream, but an objective that he fully intended to achieve.

Tim still uses the tricycle that Mike McCauliff dropped off at Cliff's Cafe fourteen years ago. His eyes still light up like they did in first grade. His parents still live in Townsend.

# CHAPTER 19

# YOU NEVER KNOW
## FALL 1997

During the final five years of my police career I became quite close to my mother. We had always been close but the passage of time seemed to draw us even closer together. I could sense time was taking its toll on her. She had lost her husband, my father, in the summer of 1989 and had lived alone in her relatively large home since that time. The aging process can be cruel. Doesn't care who you are, how much you have acquired, or how much you're loved. Time, over time, has a way of singling people out and doesn't waste time on the young most of the time. They're usually too hard to catch, and most often too strong to suffer the consequences of being on the clock. My mother, however, had been on the clock for eighty-one years by October 1996 and I could clearly sense she was growing tired. She wasn't as strong on her feet as she used to be. Blind in one eye since birth, her good eye was slowly starting to deteriorate. She was alone. Surrounded by four walls that spoke of distant pleasant memories by the family photographs that hung upon them, the voices of many people in those photos just as silent as her home had become. She had seen her parents, husband, and siblings go before her and although she never dwelled upon it, knew it was just a matter of time before she would have to follow. That's the bottom line for passing time. Everyone gets a turn to meet face to face with the ultimate equalizer.

Loneliness is just one of the many symptoms of the aging process. I didn't have to ask my mother if she was lonely, there was no need to. She would tell me from time to time that she was. She lived in the same town where I worked as Chief of Police and I would often stop by during the week to check on her, or on my way home at night to make sure she had eaten something for supper. We even shared some humor about time catching up on us, more so her than me, especially on what to do when the "Grim Reaper" came knocking on the door. She was ready with a vast variety of reasons to avoid such a meeting. Her legs and eyes weren't what they used to be, but her mind was still sharp enough to ward off this guy. She had her lines ready. Much the same as one would prepare for an unwanted door-to-door salesman. Her first approach would be simply to remain silent so the Reaper would think no one was home and have to return at a later time. A short-term remedy that temporarily guaranteed her name would be taken off the Reaper's "To Do List" for a day or two. For a time she thought about yelling "Nobody home!" through the closed front door but knew that was a dead give away. Of course she was fully aware that the knock could come at the rear door as well, so she was ready for both. We joked about other approaches.

My mother was now into her eighties and knew that time was becoming more and more of a problem as time passed by, basically because she was running out of it. She knew she couldn't go down to the market and purchase an extra slice of it. Time didn't come in slices. Couldn't be bought by the pound or gallon either. Measured yes, either by the hands on a clock or the passing of seasons, but not by solid or liquid measure, even though there's an old saying about "buying time." An expression often used when talking about a stay of execution, or raising the levee along the river to avoid a flood. Maybe "putting off the inevitable" would be a better expression. More appropriate. Trouble with time, at least with respect to human life, it always moves forward. Never back. The "Grim Reaper," aware of this fact, uses it to his advantage. In fact his very existence depends upon the advance of time. He's on the clock in every respect too, out there somewhere, lurking, looking over his list, waiting for just the right time to knock on destiny's door.

Knowing that remaining silent was only a short-term approach to her advancing time problem, my mother and I would on occasion, whenever the subject came up, discuss better options. Maybe tell the Reaper she needed to take a shower first, and then sneak out the back door. Or that the person he was looking for just left on a three-week vacation in Maine and the person he was speaking with was simply the live-in maid. One afternoon we were having lunch. I was in uniform as we sat and talked over a sandwich and a cup of tea. During the course of our conversation my mother asked me what type of weapon I carried and I told her it was a Smith & Wesson 9 millimeter semi-automatic. She then said, "I've got it. When the Grim Reaper comes knocking I'm just going to tell him my son's in here carrying a Smith & Wesson 9 millimeter semi-automatic on his hip, and he knows how to use it. So get lost!" We both laughed of course. Good parents teach their children well, no matter how old either become. Joking about the Grim Reaper was my mother's indirect way of preparing me for her death. She chose to look at her inevitable demise with a sense of humor. More so I think for me than for her. My father was the same way. The last thing he said to me before slipping into a medically induced morphine coma before he died was, "I sure hope that nurse gave me the good stuff." He said it for me, not for himself, because he knew where he was going. He wanted to make his death easy on me. What better way than joke about it. Good parents know that the only thing they'll ever do to hurt their children is to die and leave them. To help buffer the damage that death brings they often joke about their individual finality, even during the few remaining moments they have. They continue to teach by example about a subject matter that is difficult to accept and understand. My parents taught me many things, most importantly how to die. I can only hope when my turn comes I learned this lesson well.

As time went by my mother became more dependant upon me. In a sense I felt the "family reversal" of parent becoming child and child becoming parent. I came to better appreciate all that my mother had done for me, especially during my early years, when my life fully depended upon her. My mother had lived through the Great

Depression and World War II. She knew firsthand what sacrifice meant. What it was like to do without. In her pantry she had hoarded away so many packets of salt, sugar, pepper, mustard, and catsup from restaurants over the years, she could have supplied the entire United States Army with these sundries for at least six months. I asked her why she had so many packets stashed in her pantry and her answer was, "You never know." She knew all too well what it was like to go without salt, sugar, pepper, mustard, and catsup, and she was well prepared for the next Great Depression or Third World War. She was ready.

My mother lived on a fixed income. Social Security. She kept close track of her money. She didn't have much of it, but what she did have she watched over like a shepherd does his flock. She hoarded it away just like the sundry packets in her pantry. She felt she had to. Costs were always on the increase and her only monthly income from Uncle Sam didn't keep up with her rising cost of living. With her eyesight starting to falter, I took over the task of helping keep track of her money. Basically I would help her pay her bills and balance her companion savings and checking account once a month. An informal financial procedure that required limited mathematical skill that I grew to enjoy.

I would arrive at her home, usually for lunch, and she would tell me she wanted me to balance her checkbook. We'd eat lunch together and after eating I would retrieve her pocketbook that hung on her bedroom doorknob. I never knew what I'd find when I opened it to take out her checkbook. For sure there'd be a couple packets of salt or sugar from her last venture out into the world. After a while I knew enough not to ask her why she had them. She knew that I knew that she knew "You never know," so there was no point in asking. In her wallet she kept a laminated tip chart, figured in various dollar and cent increments at either 15 or 20 percent, so she could immediately know what amount to tip a waitress or waiter without having to do the math in her head. I found this rather amusing because I never knew my mother to pay a restaurant check. In fact I never heard her say,

"Let me get that," or, "This meal's on me." This wasn't one of those "You never know" situations for I did know that I always was the one to pay our check. I didn't mind. She was, after all, the woman that brought me into the world and nurtured me, so taking her out to eat was the least I could do to thank her, even if she carried a tip chart and I didn't.

Early in October I arrived at my mother's home for lunch and she asked me to help pay her bills and balance her accounts. My mother owned her own home and with the exception of real estate taxes biannually she incurred only three bills per month: electricity, telephone, and propane fuel. She had, give or take a thousand dollars, approximately twenty thousand dollars to her name. In short, tracking her finances wasn't a major task by any means. On this particular fall day I went to her bedroom door, got her pocketbook from the doorknob, and walked back to the kitchen table to assume my personal accountant duties. I opened her pocketbook to retrieve her checkbook and found a wad of cash inside, as if she were the local bookie who had just finished making the rounds. I took the money out and counted it. She had twelve hundred dollars all in twenty-dollar bills. Had someone set her up for a scam? She was elderly and I was a cop, so I asked what any son would ask regardless of profession, "Mother why do you have all this cash in your pocketbook?" I should have known what the answer would be but for some reason in this instance I never connected the dots. She didn't answer my question, more because she didn't hear me, not because she didn't have an answer. So I asked her again, "Mother, why do you have all this cash in your pocketbook?" She looked me right in the eye and very seriously responded, "I put it there because you never know." In response I asked, "You never know what, Mother?" She then said without hesitation, "Well you just never know!" I hadn't lived through the Great Depression, and World War II was over by the time I was five years old so I guess I really didn't know. How could I? I did know, however, that it wasn't safe for an elderly woman living alone to have a large sum of cash in her pocketbook hanging on her bedroom doorknob and she agreed that I should take the money to the bank and put it back into her savings account.

Feeling good that I had easily convinced her to put her cash in a safe place I continued with my unofficial accountant duties. My mother had just received her monthly social security check for $1,257. I wrote three checks from her checking account to pay her monthly bills and wrote a fourth check which would allow me to transfer six hundred dollars from her checking account to her companion savings account. This I would do the same time I deposited the twelve hundred dollars back into her savings account that she had taken out to have on hand for one of those "You never know" situations. Once my auditing was completed I read the bottom line of both accounts to my mother. "In your checking account you have $728.56 and a total of $18,257.28 in your savings account." My mother looked at me seriously and said, "You know, that social security money really adds up over time, doesn't it." Not asking me a question, but making statement of fact. She was accumulating what she felt was a small fortune and felt good about it. She had, after all, gone without during the lean years and was now, at least in her own mind, "well healed." She openly expressed her happiness by telling me how good she felt having so much money in the bank. I told her I was proud of her and asked, "What do plan on doing with all that money?" She became serious again and said, "I'll just save it for a rainy day." "Well," I said, "maybe you might want to spend some of it on yourself. Maybe buy a new dress or get your hair done." "No," she said, "I'm just going to leave it in the bank." "Why?" I asked. I should have known. "You never know," she replied.

# AFTERMATH:

My mother passed away in June of 2000 after living a full life. Her only extravagance was love. That I do know.

# CHAPTER 20

# THE WOOD SPLITTER
## FALL 1996

Roy Shepherd, the same person who worked with me attempting to save Sean Coffey, grew up on a farm in Townsend and graduated from high school two years before I did. We never really got to know each other during our youth because Roy lived on the outskirts of town while I lived almost in the exact center. Plus Roy was a farm boy and if he weren't in school he'd be working alongside his father helping out with the many chores that went with the territory. In addition to harvesting crops and taking care of animals, Roy received a pretty good education in mechanical engineering. During his youth he got to know all about different types of machinery, fixing things when they were broken, and operating them when they weren't. While most kids his age played Little League baseball, Roy was driving the family tractor, and if it broke he fixed that too. He didn't know it at the time but the mechanical skills he learned early on would take him far from the farm and into the lives of many people in desperate need.

During the 1970s the Townsend ambulance was operated solely by police officers that were trained in basic first aid and volunteered their time. I became the first full-time certified emergency medical technician to work in Townsend in June of 1974. As the community began to grow so did the need for both police and emergency medical services. The handwriting was on the wall. The police department could not continue to fulfill both demands. As a result, I successfully "opened up" the ambulance service to anyone in the community that wanted to serve and was willing to qualify at their own expense for the training required. The transition took a few years and the ambulance service became a separate department. Roy, a volunteer firefighter, had successfully completed the necessary training for emergency medical technician certification, and became Director of the Townsend Ambulance Service.

Roy and I had worked closely over the years, our common thread, emergency services. He owned and operated a small business that specialized in the sale and repair of lawn mowers and snow blowers. He also continued to operate the family farm as well. Roy was one of those hard working individuals who crammed thirty hours of getting things done into a twenty-four hour day. His pick-up truck was equipped with an emergency radio, an assortment of various tools, and most important, an individual trained in emergency medical response that had an in-depth knowledge of how machines functioned. I had responded to a couple of emergency calls for men with their hands caught in snow blowers and Roy was right there with me. I tended to the medical needs of victims while Roy dismantled the machines enough to get the victims free and into a waiting ambulance. Roy operated an auto body shop as well, and he brought his dual medical and mechanical skills to automobile crash sites to help free victims trapped in wreckages. Roy knew exactly what do, and just as important, what not to do. There wasn't anything mechanical he couldn't figure out. The amazing part, he did it all in seconds. How well an accident victim is medically treated within the first hour of trauma is directly related to their survivability. If the process takes too long the end result could be longer recovery, permanent injury, or death. The sixty-minute game of beat the clock starts right from the moment the emergency occurs.

I was sitting in my police cruiser in the back lot of the police station one October afternoon in 1996 when I received a radio call advising me to go to a home on Smith Street for a man caught in a wood splitter. My trained response was immediate and I activated my emergency blue lights and siren. I calculated that I was about one minute from the scene and started to think about what I was heading into. Wood splitter? Where in the wood splitter was the man stuck? What was stuck? Clothing? Body part? I had never had an emergency wood splitter call before but based upon my snow blower and lawn mower emergency experience, assumed most likely it was a hand. I heard my telecommunicator dispatch an ambulance right after alerting me to the emergency so I figured "body part" was a given. Just before I radioed out of my car at the scene I heard Roy Shepherd sign on over the emergency radio network and acknowledge he was on his way. Halleluiah! The Lord and Master of Mending Mechanical Disaster had mounted up and was on his way to save the day! I didn't know how bad the situation was yet but was about to quickly find out.

I arrived at the scene and grabbed my emergency medical jump kit and quickly got out of my car. An adult male was standing next to a large hydraulic wood splitter and another younger male was sitting on the ground next to the machine. The machine had stalled and the older male couldn't get it to restart. The man on the ground had his right hand crushed completely across his palm where the fingers join the hand. His crushed hand was wedged about a half inch into one end of a twenty-two inch long log about ten inches in diameter, sandwiched in place by the V-shaped vertical metal splitting plate on one side and the semi-split piece of wood on the other, which was being held in the closed position by the flat hydraulic push plate used to compress the wood on the opposite end. I could feel the pain the young man was suffering just by looking at his trapped hand. There was some bleeding but it appeared that although his hand was crushed his fingers were still attached. He was screaming for me to get him out. He kept yelling, "For Christ sakes get me the f--- out of here, get me the f--- out of here," his last "out of here" trailing off with a loud crying moan. I yelled to the other guy to try and restart the engine in hopes that if it did we could back off the hydraulic cylinder and free the hand. He tried but the engine wouldn't start. The young man grimacing in pain then yelled, "Shoot me for Christ sakes, shoot me." "Look," I yelled back, "I'm not going to shoot you. I'm going to get you out of this real quick, but you have to work with me." I could tell he wasn't listening to me by what he yelled next. "If you can't do it then give me your f---ing gun so I can do it myself." With that I got right in his face making sure my service weapon was out of reach of his usable hand and yelled back, "No one is going to shoot anyone! Get that out of your head! Understand!" Looking directly into his eyes to affirm that my use of the word "understand" was not being put to him in the form of a question but forcefully as a plan of action. To reaffirm my position I told him again, "We're going to get you out of this mess."

Roy Shepherd pulled up and ran over to where we were. I quickly explained the situation to him but I doubted he needed my input. He could plainly see the problem we were facing. He made two quick attempts to start the engine without success. With that he ran over to his truck and came back with a large adjustable wrench and a short crowbar. He ran the crowbar as best he could into the tightest part of the semi-split wood so once the pressure was released the wood wouldn't pinch down harder on the victim's hand. He then took the adjustable wrench and loosened one end of the black hydraulic hose that ran to the splitting piston. With the hydraulic pressure relieved he manually reversed the direction of the piston compression plate and freed the victim's hand. The victim, still in pain but relieved to be free, was transported in the Townsend ambulance to the hospital.

## AFTERMATH:

Investigation showed the victim was nineteen years old and lived in Fitchburg, Massachusetts, but was helping his friend in Townsend when the accident happened. He was treated for multiple fractures of his right hand, did not lose any of his fingers, and was released from the hospital the following day. I called him at home shortly thereafter to see how he was doing. In the course of our conversation I asked him what size shoes he wore and told him I wanted to stop by and talk to him about what had happened. The following day I went to visit him and found he was living alone in a low-end apartment. When he came to the door his right hand was heavily bandaged and held up by a sling. As I expected he came to the door wearing just socks on his feet. I knew I would find him like this because in 1988 I had severely cut two fingers on my right hand with my table saw which left me with a temporary inability to tie my shoes. As we stood talking in the doorway he related the amount of pain he was still in and was frustrated by the fact he couldn't tie his shoes, therefore he wasn't wearing any. I told him I understood his plight and handed him a new pair of Velcro-strapped sneakers I had purchased for him, explaining how easy they were to put on one-handed. With tears in his eyes he asked me to thank those who helped him and thanked me for the sneakers.

Roy Shepherd had again combined emergency medical and mechanical skills not often seen in field. He knew exactly how to release the pressure on that wood splitter as well as ensure the wood being split wouldn't compress harder on the victim's hand once the initial pressure was released. He could have done it blindfolded, in the dark, or upside down for that matter. He was the best. Roy would continue to respond to help people in need. Not just those caught up in emergency situations but those who simply needed a hand. He is retired now and spends his time doing things around the farm surrounded by his family and a community that loves him. Over the years I've become a good judge of character. Roy Shepherd is one of those special people, a product of good parents, strong discipline, proper schooling, Yankee ingenuity, and an oversized heart.

I never saw or heard from the victim again. I heard he had recovered quite well from the injuries he received and has partial use of his right hand. The last I knew he was living in Maine.

# CHAPTER 21

# HILLARY RODHAM CLINTON
## FALL 2007

I had been retired five years and was sitting in my recliner in my living room after supper one October evening when the telephone rang. My wife Jeanne answered and I couldn't help but hear her side of the conversation. "Yes, this is Jeanne May," she said. I listened while my wife continued to speak with the unknown person on the other end. "Hillary, fantastic!" she exclaimed. I sat in my chair thinking "Hillary?" I knew plenty of women named Donna, Mary, and Susan. I even knew one named Martha, and another named Irma, but I couldn't think of anyone I knew named Hillary. Sure there was Senator Hillary Clinton, campaigning for President of the United States. That was the only Hillary that came to mind and I knew she wouldn't be calling our house. I felt certain whoever was on the other end of the line wasn't Hillary Clinton telling my wife she was coming over for a cup of tea, so I just sat wondering, "Who could this Hillary person be?" The conversation continued. "Oh I'm so sorry. I can't make it on Wednesday, but my husband can." Now my mind was really starting to turn. "His first name is William," my wife continued, "last name May. May just like the month. May. Okay, I'll spell it for you, M-A-Y." Now I knew I was in trouble. I didn't know who Hillary was on the other end but felt she couldn't be very smart. I had the spelling of my last name down by first grade and here was this Hillary person who couldn't even spell my last name correctly. Sure I could understand the need to spell it out if my last name was Wojuilewicz, or even Solvenkia for that matter, but it wasn't. It was May! Not June or April, one or two steps up the ladder of difficulty, just May, plain and simple. I continued to listen becoming more concerned. "Go to the table marked 'M through P' no later than two-thirty on Wednesday afternoon the 7th. Fine, he'll be there. Thank you so much for the call."

My wife hung up the phone went to our bedroom and came back holding a book. "You'll never guess who that was on the phone," she said with a sense of excitement in her voice. Before I could take a stab at it she continued, "That was Hillary Clinton's campaign office. Hillary," my wife went on to say as if she knew her on a personal level, "is going to hold a Town Hall meeting in Peterborough, New Hampshire on November 7th and she invited me to go, but I have to work. So I told them you could make it. The meeting starts at three in the afternoon. You have to be there no later than two-thirty. Go to the table marked 'M though P' to pick up your ticket and clear security." My wife then held out the book she was holding, "Living History" by Hillary Rodham Clinton, and handed it to me. "While you're there," she said, "have Hillary sign my book for me." "What!" I exclaimed, "I won't get anywhere near Hillary Clinton let alone have her sign your book. What are you crazy?" My wife looked at me for a moment and then said, "No, I'm not crazy. If anybody can get my book signed by Hillary it's you. You can do it." That statement confirmed my true belief, she wasn't crazy, she was insane!

Talk about pressure. Time passed by. As the 7th drew nearer I hoped that maybe pneumonia or some other sickness would have me bedridden for a few days. I needed an honest excuse to prevent me from going to see Hillary, and I knew the usual "headache" wouldn't work. By the evening of the 6th I knew a miracle just wasn't going to happen. I had been brought up Catholic and believed in miracles! Where was God when I needed him? I tried as best possible to psych myself up for the 7th, which in my mind became known as "Hillary Day." Most men have just one big day to worry about in life, Valentines Day. Forget that little baby and things can get real miserable real quick, and the suffering can last for weeks. Now I had another one, "Hillary Day!"

The 7th arrived right on schedule with a beautiful sunrise. Just the kind of day best suited for working in the yard or going for a hike. I would have felt better if it was raining. Rainy days and meetings seemed to go hand in hand, meant for each other. The autograph game was on whether I liked it or not, so I got ready to head out for the most difficult task imaginable, getting Hillary to sign my wife's book. Before leaving my house I took a three-by-five card and printed my wife's name "JEANNE" on it in bold block letters using a dark blue marker pen. If in fact there was a miracle, even though my first in the form of an illness never happened, the last thing I needed was to have Hillary spell my wife's name incorrectly should the second extraordinary event actually occur. After all they were on a first name basis, so I figured having my wife's name "ready to be spelled correctly" was a brilliant move on my part. Plus I liked the color of dark blue. Warm to a certain degree yet appearing bold and strong by the little extra width created by the felt tip. If I had been famous this would have been how I would have signed my name. Ready to go, I put the card inside the book, the pen in my jacket pocket, and headed out the door to hopefully meet Hillary.

I arrived in Peterborough and had to park four blocks from the Town Hall. The place was a mob scene. As I made my way through the crowd I noticed I was the only one carrying Hillary's book. In fact I was the only person carrying a book! Interesting. I got in line for the 'M through P' people and was handed a short form to fill out. I finally got to the official 'M through P' greeter, handed her my completed form and was impressed to learn my name was on her list. With that she handed me an admission ticket and said, "Have a nice day Mister May." Poetic justice? Not really. "Have a nice day Mister Slovenkia," same thing really. Sure she meant what she said but "nice day" under the circumstances was stretching sincerity to just short of the breaking point. With that I walked through the front door of the Town Hall, handed my ticket to a true-blooded American Democrat, and headed into the meeting hall. I worked my way to the far left and found a seat on the far outside about sixteen rows back. Not a very good location for a one-on-one discussion with Hillary, but with such a large crowd was the best I could do. Plus there was a metal fence barricade set up in front of the stage, so any chance of me getting within arms length of Senator Clinton was slim at best. In addition I noticed Secret Service agents standing in the front. They all looked the same with their dark suits, business neckties, stern looks, wired earplugs, and little coded lapel buttons. I sat and waited while trying to figure out how I could possibly overcome all these obstacles in my quest for an autograph.

On stage there were two comfy stuffed chairs and a podium. The hall was filled to standing room only when a gentleman took the stage to a welcoming round of applause. He looked familiar to me but I couldn't place him. He greeted everyone, introduced himself as "Bob Vila," famous for his public television show "This Old House," and started to talk about the rising costs of owning a home, thus setting the theme for the meeting. To the far right of the stage behind a large blue curtain, obscure from the view of most present, I could see Hillary Clinton waiting to come on stage. Behind her there was an exit door. This concerned me because I knew after her talk she would quickly leave out this doorway into a waiting vehicle and quickly disappear along with any chance of me getting my wife's book signed. The possibility of me making my way through the crowd, walking around the building, and then past security seemed next to impossible. I decided to do what I always did when I didn't know what to do, nothing.

Bob Vila introduced Hillary to a thunderous round of applause. Bob asked her well-scripted questions upon which she gave informative answers. Her presentation lasted about an hour and concluded with another round of loud and lasting applause as she exited the stage. I stood up like everyone else trying to determine my next move, which had become restricted. The crowd was moving toward the rear doors of the hall when I looked back to the stage area and saw Hillary still standing behind the curtain. Unbeknownst to most she hadn't left the building. I stayed at my seat pondering my next move. I knew I couldn't get through the crowd in the rear quick enough to get to Hillary before she got into a waiting vehicle and I also knew I would be quickly arrested if I went beyond the metal fence barricade in front of me. So I just stood and watched what Hillary was doing behind the curtain. For most everyone there the show was over, but for me there was still hope. Slim at best, but as long as I could see Hillary I still had a chance.

Then something unbelievable happened. Hillary came out from behind the curtain and started working the crowd on the inside of the metal fence barricade. I immediately made my way to the front of the hall and squeezed between two people standing in front of the barricade. They both gave me dirty looks but I was on a mission like no other. I knew I'd never see them again but I had to live with my wife the rest of my life. The mood was joyous yet politically reserved, with handshakes and discussions between Hillary and her constituents. She was slowly moving in my direction. I couldn't believe it. Just moments before all hope had seemed lost. Now I sensed opportunity would be knocking at my door, and I wasn't about to ask, "Who's there?" I was ready to throw that door open and say, "Hello Hillary, I can guarantee you two votes if you sign my wife's book!" She was a Washington insider so I figured I'd use the politically successful "You rub my back and I'll rub yours" approach. I didn't know if Hillary would make it to me because I was on the far side of the hall, but as time went by she got closer. When she was standing two people to my right I figured I'd get ready for "the signing." I knew she was pressed for time and I wanted everything ready for her, so I reached inside my jacket for the pen. As I pulled my hand out of my pocket I felt someone grab my wrist. So hard I couldn't move my arm any further. I turned my head and saw this large guy wearing bib overalls, flannel shirt with matching cap, who appeared to have just come off the farm. He told me, "If she wants to sign that book she'll use her own pen. Put that back in your pocket and keep your hands out of your pockets. Understand!" He wasn't asking me if I understood, he was telling me I had better. So I just said, "Yes sir." I had never seen a Secret Service agent dressed as a farmer before. I immediately developed a new respect for both.

With book in hand along with my "JEANNE" three-by-five card plainly visible, I waited. Hillary engaged in serious conversation with the lady to my immediate right, shook her hand, thanked her for her support and then sidestepped and faced me directly. The mood continued to be professional and courteous, yet serious. Looking Hillary right in the eye I said, "Good morning Senator Clinton. My name is Bill May. If you sign your book for my wife I won't have to wipe dishes for a whole month." Hillary busted out with laughter, almost as if she needed a break from tradition. So did everyone else. Hillary looked me right in the eye and said, "Well Bill May I'm going to make you one happy man," and while surrounded by laughter took the book from my hand and signed the inside cover, "To Jeanne, Hillary Rodham Clinton." We exchanged pleasantries and she continued to the next person waiting in line.

## AFTERMATH:

Perhaps the most gratifying aspect of this event was that I didn't have to execute "Plan Two" with respect to "Hillary Day." My second fail-safe strategy that I developed which would have ensured Hillary's signature appeared inside the front cover of the book regardless of how close I had gotten to her. I knew Hillary would be surrounded by security and that the chance of me being able to get within twenty feet of her was minimal at best, which meant my chance for getting her to sign the book was even less promising. I had conceived a second method to acquire her signature should my first plan fail, one that guaranteed success. On the outside front of the dustcover of the book, just below Senator Clinton's photograph, appeared her signature. Not a real autograph but printed on during the production process, so it appeared as if she had actually signed it. My second plan was to copy this signature by inscribing the inside of the cover of my wife's book just like Hillary had, including the Jeanne part. In fact I had practiced doing this a few times on scrap paper along with a special message which included "To my good friend Jeanne" but figured that was stretching it a bit, so I stuck with just "To Jeanne," which ironically was the exact way Hillary signed her book. Since "Plan One" had worked flawlessly I didn't have to implement "Plan Two," which would have made me a forger of the lowest form. Bad enough signing someone else's name, there was also the deceit of passing it off as real, to my wife no less. Get caught doing something like that and its one strike I'm out, not three. I felt good knowing I had done the right thing even though Hillary was the one who did it, not me. Knowing the signature inside my wife's copy of "Living History" was an original, not fake. Placed there by Senator Hillary Clinton herself. I could imagine sitting cloaked in guilt as my wife showed her friends a phony autographed book while expressing her pride in my great accomplishment. I could imagine five generations from now one of my decedents appearing on Antique Road Show only to learn their one thousand dollar treasure was only worth five bucks because some bum had forged the signature. Thanks to Hillary I wouldn't have to spend the rest of my life knowing I was that bum. I felt good knowing I could go to bed with peace of mind while an actual signed copy of "Living History" sat on my wife's bed stand.

Senator Hillary Clinton was not elected President of the United States. I'm back wiping dishes. In a sense we both lost. My only mistake, I should have told Senator Clinton if she signed the book I wouldn't have to wipe dishes for the rest of my life, but in the excitement of our encounter I just wasn't thinking correctly.

# CLOSING REMARKS

So there you have it, a brief look into the life of a small town police officer. Brief in the sense that I selected only a few short stories to tell among the many that occurred over a thirty-year career. Not that those excluded were any less significant than those mentioned here because they weren't, it's just that allowable space, much like time, dictates the final outcome. I could have written volumes detailing the disastrous circumstances I witnessed firsthand, and for those I've included within this text I chose to be brief in their story lines for two reasons. First, to spare survivors of those tragedies the pain of reliving their misfortune by providing pages of detailed information that serves no useful purpose now. What they had to endure. What they still live with. Second, as subjective as it may seem, for the same reason as the first. I do not like going back there either, although there are times when I have no choice. Like it or not, this book is based on fact, and the fact of the matter is, these events, and many more, actually occurred in Townsend, Massachusetts during my tenure as a police officer there from 1973 to 2002. I did not write this partial synopsis to chronicle bits and pieces of my police career, however, for truly there is a much greater story, something much larger to focus on, much greater than self. First, there were victims, good people forever lost. Taken from our world not by choice most often, but by circumstances beyond their control. Victims in the purest form, their suffering the end product of someone else's viciousness, malcontent, bad judgment, or nature's will. I say most often because there were some who chose to take their own life. In those cases, whatever the reasoning or lack thereof, they too are among the lost. All of them good people, who left those who loved them only to ask, "Why?"

Importantly, there were the children; their shortened life spans chronicled upon their headstones. Someone once told me that it wasn't the first or final date etched into a gravestone that mattered, what counted most was what someone achieved between those dates. One might think this standard should not apply to children, for the numbers engraved upon their grave markers do not speak to a lifetime fulfilled. How can they be judged in such a way? I would submit they should be and provide this answer. During their shortened stay they gave our world something in short supply and desperately needed; love. What greater gift can any person give to another? What greater legacy? To me it's not what was achieved between dates of existence that matter; it's what was given back that's meaningful, regardless of how much or little time was allowed. We can learn from children, even in death. They can teach us what caring means, especially during those early years, when truthfulness and honesty are just a normal way of life. They can show us the pathway to greatness, one that adults sometimes stray from during life's journey. All we have to do is look to them for direction and true meaning. Imagine living in a world built upon a foundation of a child's love.

Second, there were the many survivors, hundreds not even mentioned within these pages, caught up in happenings they never expected they would have to face during their lifetime. Yet they did, with tremendous strength and dignity. These people are unique, for within their own individual struggle they openly displayed the best possible course to take to survive. When faced with no place to turn other than their God or inner self, they chose to do better, to be a better person, to make the world a better place, and in doing so provided us with direction to follow should crisis ever unexpectedly arrive on our doorstep.

Lastly, there were the emergency responders I worked alongside, who actively or passively, went about the task of trying to turn wrong into right. Even in the face of overwhelming odds they vigorously continued to work together toward common goals that sometimes went unattained. Not because they didn't know how to achieve their objectives, they did, but on some occasions it made no difference how much knowledge or skill was placed on the scale of accomplishment, forces beyond human ability often outweighed the expertise applied, tilting the scale toward unwanted conclusions. To show the depth of despair that some people went through, victims as well as caregivers, I had to set forth some facts. Not as they appeared on the front page of the newspaper or were broadcast on the evening news, but by what I observed behind the scenes and by what survivors have told me. Do not be mistaken; this is not about any one person or sensationalizing the past. This is about trying to desensitize difficult memories, defined quite simply as post-traumatic stress disorder.

The human mind is an extraordinary control center. Information passes through it at lightening speed. Data can be sorted and stored away within it faster than the modern day computer. What the mind doesn't have, with the exception of some that are diseased or damaged, is a "delete key." Stop for a moment and think of your very first memory. How far back, in years, did that take you? Was it a happy thought? Isn't it amazing that you were able to sort through endless amounts of data stored inside your brain, go chronologically to the bottom of the list, and instantly come up with your very first recollection? Now ask yourself this simple question. What does two plus two equal? You immediately knew the answer was four as soon as you finished reading the question. Again you were able to instantly sort through endless amounts of information within your mind to produce the correct result. Your intellectual journey most likely took you back to grammar school where you first learned simple mathematics, or perhaps to a special someone who trained you at an early age. While seeking the answer "four," however, you didn't think about who might have taught you what two plus two equaled or where you learned it. You went directly to the answer without any "side trips" along the way. Your response was immediate and conditioned.

Now here is the difficult part. Totally forget that two plus two equals four. Get that memory completely out of your head. Try to rid yourself of that answer four. Can't do it? You're not alone. Certainly you can file it away and go onto other thoughts, but if someone were to again ask you what two plus two equaled guess what's going to immediately pop into your head? Four!

This easy exercise clearly demonstrates that the brain is capable of readily sorting through data with relative ease and filing it away with the same efficiency. Of equal importance, this simple math problem not only demonstrated that the only thing necessary to retrieve the answer was some type of mental trigger, but also plainly shows what the brain cannot do. Delete it. Not being able to delete within one's own head isn't a problem either until the mind records data that troubles the human spirit. The inability to delete malignant matters of the mind can become overwhelming for some people trained in professions that require them to respond to, and manage, the unthinkable. Those who must work within and gather the details of the horrific events they faced head-on during the course of their "normal" workday. Filed away in either electronic form or hard copy, personal observations reduced to writing can be deleted or shredded whenever desired. This holds true for digital imaging and video documentation as well. In the real world these images can be burned or erased into oblivion. Regretfully, in these instances, the human mind cannot perform this function. There is no button to push to permanently destroy horrific history stored inside the head. I would suggest this might explain to some extent why some people commit suicide. I say to some extent, because alcohol played a major role in approximately sixty-five percent of the cases I investigated involving people who took their own life. Sadly, pushing this ultimate delete key not only destroyed unwanted images within the mind, but the good imagery as well, let alone the body. This inability to delete might offer some insight into alcoholism as well. If you can't delete it, just fog it over.

Even after being retired ten years there are still triggers that bring back memories I wish I could avoid. Of significance, in my case, I knew many of my victims. They had personalities attached to their human existence. They had names, faces and family. They were part of my community. Some were friends. There isn't a street in my hometown that doesn't hold a bad memory for me. Often many. Exact locations, such as houses and specific sections of roadway are guaranteed triggers. There are other things. Simple things. Anniversary dates. Names. Clothing. Seasons. There are times when tragic memories can knock you down. Often when least expected. I survived in my profession by telling myself that good things happened too. This book is a partial synopsis of my career, the good coexisting with the bad. Not a good mix really, but I couldn't choose the ingredients, arrival times, or the packages they came in.

Sadly, tragically, I led investigations into seven homicide cases during my thirty-year career in a community of less than nine thousand. My youngest victim was a two-month old boy. When the child wouldn't stop crying his father threw him against a bedroom wall. I went to Missouri to arrest him and aided in his prosecution that sent him to prison. My oldest murder victim was in her middle eighties. Her name was Mary Bell, killed by her elderly brother who struck her three times in the head with an axe while she was sleeping. I knew the precise number of blows she received to her head because Edward Bell told me the exact amount when I arrested him. The blood splatter evidence left by the axe on the bedroom ceiling confirmed his statement. He killed her because he feared there would be no one to take care of her when he died. After his arrest he was confined at Worcester State Mental Hospital where I would occasionally pick him up for court appearances. On our return trip back to the hospital I would stop and buy him a chocolate chip cone at an ice cream stand along the way. His favorite. Certainly he had committed a despicable act according to criminal law, but was he responsible for his actions? Did he truly understand the wrong he had done? In his time-ravaged mind he helped his sister, not hurt her. He killed her because he loved her. During our "road trips" we became friends. He died at the hospital. I didn't realize how alone in the world this man was until I attended his wake. I was the only one there. I left with a better understanding of his despair.

The last murder case I oversaw involved the shooting of a young male by three of his companions in April of 2002. Although murdered in Townsend they removed his body to a residential cul-de-sac in a neighboring community where they doused the remains with gasoline and set it ablaze. Ironically, one fingerprint was not destroyed in the inferno, which led to an early identification of the deceased, and quickly to those involved. All three were convicted. One was a young mother of two children. The case still moves through the judicial system as one defendant has recently won an appeal for a new trial ten years after the murder was committed.

I worked investigations into a vast number of other deaths classified as manslaughter, motor vehicle homicide, accidental, suicide, or death by natural causes. Approximately one hundred suicides and an equal number of motor vehicle deaths occurred during my career. When the legal age for alcohol consumption was lowered from twenty-one to eighteen in 1983, the number of motor vehicle deaths rose dramatically. Not until it was raised to twenty-one again in 1986 did the numbers start to fall. Each death brought the pain that only those who loved the victims can feel, and tragically never understand, for they too became victims. A rational mind cannot make sense of senseless acts. Even when all the pieces fit, when the reason for death can be explained, the mind doesn't want to accept it.

One of my hardest jobs was notifying parents that their son or daughter had just been killed in a tragic car crash. I've been there. I've done it. More times than I want to remember, but still do. Reactions of mothers in this terrible situation varied from one extreme to the other. Some simply stood with a passive stare, while others immediately struck out in anger with closed fists not wanting to believe. I just stood and took the first couple of blows to my chest and then grabbed their wrists. In no way an act of courage, simply my small way of helping a mother absorb the horrible pain I had just delivered. I grew to understand and accept both types of behavior, as well as any reaction in between, as appropriate responses for the unbearable. The same held true for fathers as well, who often appeared "lost" when told his child was dead. There is no correct way to receive or process the death of a child, your child. How can there be a right way for something so wrong? There is an unwanted finality to death. Hopes and dreams for happy tomorrows are shattered by this one occurrence. Subconsciously, individuals think an exception will be made in their case, only to ask "Now what?" when it happens. There is no immediate answer for "Now what?" Sometimes there is never an answer.

Working in a dual capacity as police officer and emergency medical technician I witnessed people of all ages die while attempting to apply every medical means I knew to save their life. I often did this alongside other emergency service responders in full view of at least one parent or close relative. I also delivered emergency death notifications from other jurisdictions and was responsible for making positive identification of the deceased. Age made no difference. I came to know death on a very personal level. Not as a friend. I didn't enjoy our relationship. I despised death. Never knowing when it would show up next or how it would arrive. How I wanted to sever our connection, but we were linked by profession.

I have total recall of every murder, fatal motor vehicle accident, common fatal accident, suicide, and natural death scene I responded to and investigated over a thirty-year period. I can quickly bring into focus numbers and types of wounds, their locations, colors of hair, victims clothing right down to buttons or logos, and the condition of bodies when found. I can go back and review each of them as if there were hundreds of memory sticks stacked within my brain. Just a simple click of my mental mouse and my mind can instantly recreate scenes from the past, image after image. They're all still there. Stored away. Serving no useful purpose now. The only exceptions, three unsolved mysteries that still remain. The brutal murder of schoolteacher Judith Viewig in May of 1973 and the disappearance of thirteen-year-old Debora Quimby in May of 1977. The third is the March 1985 murder of Edward Gokey. Not a mystery to me, for I have a good understanding of those responsible for his death. One is now deceased himself. Having a good understanding, however, doesn't reach the threshold of 'proof beyond all reasonable doubt' needed to convict. This case, like the other two, simply need that final piece of the puzzle before they can be brought before a Grand Jury to seek indictments for those responsible. Time and new technology may lead to success. These three cases are still open, actively worked on, and I remain prepared to testify when necessary.

I also worked closely with the Middlesex County District Attorney's Office on a serial murder case in which the convicted offender grew up in Townsend and was well known to me. I know every detail of the methods he used to kill his female victims in another jurisdiction. Good women who went along with him because he held a knife to their throats. Perhaps they felt if they did as they were told they would be released unharmed. We'll never know. They can't tell us. They're dead. His motivation was anger, his weakness alcohol. His youngest victim was only fourteen years old, and like the others was sexually assaulted. The last living thing she did was cry while asking to go home to her mother. He told her she could as long as she took a shower before he dropped her off in the area of where she was originally kidnapped. While her back was turned in the shower stall he strangled her with a telephone cord. He is serving a life sentence without any possibility of parole in a Virginia prison. To be very candid, when it comes to death and dying there isn't much I haven't seen, heard, or recorded in my mind.

I know by telling this story I have exposed old wounds. People do not want to be reminded. Clearly that was not my intent in writing this book. With the exception of close survivors, some who worked directly with me putting this book together, I certainly know how most people in my hometown feel. Probably more so, I went where they didn't have to go. I would hope that I am not judged by what some will say is an exception to the rule. The Gustafson murders remain one of the most heinous crimes committed in Massachusetts during the 20th century. It was, and still remains, an exception to the rule. I didn't set that standard, the killer did. I offer that as a matter of fact, and not an attempt on my part to ward off any criticism for my choice of subject matter in this writing. Further, there were many other tragic cases that occurred during my tenure of equal importance, but it isn't the magnitude of any one event that sets the bar. If you were to ask me which incident was the most heartbreaking over the years I would have to answer they all were. Each deeply impacted those involved, and as such, left their imprint on me. Limitations beyond my control restrict the amount of case histories I can put forth.

Mixing the good with the bad was just the way things chronologically happened. Everyone has moments of joy and sadness, but on my job I traveled to the highest of highs and the lowest of lows on a regular basis. For the most part, tragic stories that make the headlines are quickly forgotten, or so we assume. This invalid assumption is disconcerting, a result in part, of our fast-paced lifestyle. After all, there is a new day with a new story that shadows the old. In most cases the bad news receives precedence over the good, intentionally placed in that order to capture immediate attention. News seems to run in twenty-four hour cycles unless your name appears on the front page or television screen. Once that happens you take ownership and the story never ends. The "this too shall pass" philosophy ceases to exist. "Good press" is often built on "bad news." Certainly the need to know is important, but the need to understand runs much deeper, especially with victims. New news gets old real fast and quickly fades away, leaving survivors to linger on, often forgotten in the process.

The destructive force of wrong and evil in this world goes far beyond what I witnessed. I was only one among the many. There are cities and towns across our country where men and women set about the task of responding to the unforeseen crisis that requires their immediate attention. They can't say, or even think for that matter, "Well I'll take care of that in a minute or two." Highly educated in their respective fields, their response is automatic, immediate, and calculated. These workers number in the hundreds of thousands. They do their job and go home when their workday is over most of the time. Regretfully some die in the line of duty. Those who are fortunate return to their families but often bring their work home with them. Tucked inside their head, not a briefcase. They might tell their significant other about the overall picture but won't go into detail. This is quite understandable. Why burden someone close to you with the unthinkable? This "close it out" approach can, over time, take its toll on the emergency caregiver because it also "locks it in."

During a recent project I was working on I met a young volunteer firefighter. He told me about a rescue call he had responded to where a factory worker had been crushed to death by a piece of heavy equipment. The rescue crew he was assigned to was also responsible for removing the man's body. He told me <u>unsolicited</u> that the thing he remembered most about the incident was seeing the deceased man's boots sticking out from under the machine that had crushed the victim. He went on to describe the boots in detail and mentioned how he even dreams about them. I asked him how long he had been a firefighter. He told me just a few years. I also asked if there had been a post-incident stress debriefing after the event and he advised there hadn't. To me his remarks represented a classic example of the beginning stages of post-traumatic stress, and sadly, what wasn't done to help manage it. As I stood talking with him I wondered how many traumatic events it would take to bring him down. I recommended he talk with a professional counselor about what he had witnessed and he told me he was "doing fine." Think about it. Dreaming about a dead man's boots is not "doing fine." Post-traumatic stress can be like blowing up a balloon over an extended period of time. One breath, then another, and over time the balloon gets bigger. At some point the balloon can't withstand further inhalations and goes to pieces. A pair of boots this month, maybe a bloodied jacket or a child's broken body the next, ongoing over time until the mind can't absorb any more tragic images and the human spirit collapses. I would suggest there is an "add on" effect in many post-traumatic stress cases. I know in my case it took seventeen years and many shocking events before the bad news balloon inside my brain couldn't handle any further expansion.

Positive self-analysis is often presented metaphorically as looking at your glass as being half full rather than half empty. I had held true to this belief for many years. I am nothing more than a retired cop. My level of medical training is limited to satisfying the requirements for certification as an emergency medical technician. I am not a doctor, clinician, or psychologist. I did however survive thirty years working within the wreckage of people's lives and would suggest that post-traumatic stress disorder is not an abnormal condition of the mind. In fact it is nothing more than having normal reactions to very abnormal events. I used the plural form in that last sentence, but one significant event can put you on the P.T.S.D. team real quick, and you don't have to work in the emergency service field either. Just one event can make you the star player. Post-traumatic stress goes beyond looking at whether your glass is half full or half empty. Regardless of the level inside your glass, the more significant question has to be, "How heavy is it?" If you hold the glass for a minute it may not seem too heavy. What if you have to hold it for an hour? A day? A year? Ten years? Seventeen, like I did? There comes a time when the glass becomes so heavy you have to put it down. What if you don't realize it, or if you do, you can't seem to be able to? What happens if there is more than one glass? Say three for instance and you only have two hands. How about a few hundred?

This book is for those people who know their glass is half full, or even half empty for that matter, but don't often understand what their glass contains, or how heavy it can become. Those who have gone into, or continued to participate in emergency response situations, performing flawlessly because they have a trained ability to block out the victim's persona and get down to the gruesome business at hand. If they are fortunate they attended a mandatory post-incident stress-debriefing meeting before being allowed to leave work, or within a short period of time thereafter. They were given an opportunity to put that heavy glass down, even if just for a moment. They had occasion to learn they weren't alone in their terrible thoughts because co-workers had similar feelings. They were given a chance to rid themselves of the "what ifs," and the "only ifs" that come with the territory. They were able to vent their anger that is often part of the package, especially in the death of a child. They grew to realize that grown men and women actually do cry, and yes, they cry together. They left work knowing they made the best possible difference under the extreme circumstances presented. They came to realize that sometimes there are powers far greater than that of any man or woman that dictates the outcome of a tragic event. Sadly some workplaces still do not provide post-incident stress-debriefing sessions for their workers. Some employers do not agree that stress debriefings actually provide any good purpose. Some say they cannot afford to pay for them. Perhaps offering them on a volunteer basis would be a good place to start. I can only say stress debriefings worked for me during the last ten years of my career and wonder how much better I would have survived on a personal level if they had existed during my first twenty years on the job.

I want to bring awareness to a problem that is buried from public view. One that is often spoken about in hushed tones. Or at times joked about, even in the field. Not that P.T.S.D. is funny, but simply because "happy hides hurt." Medical professionals have to honor patient confidentiality. What is discussed in the privacy of the examination room stays there. Emergency workers, because of their professional "all strong, all knowing" images, always present themselves as being in complete command. Having a troubled mind brings with it a connotation of loss of control. Certainly a quality you hope not to find in a person given exclusive power to manage crisis situations, especially someone wearing a loaded gun on their hip. With that mindset the rationale is to hide the truth. How do I know that? Simple. I did it for many years. I tried to convince those around me, as well as myself, that I could walk in and out of human destruction the same way I walked in and out of a shower. Over time I found out I couldn't. I was amazed to learn through professional counseling that I had a very normal mind. What wasn't ordinary was the type of work I had chosen to do.

Here is what I believe based on thirty years of experience. Post-traumatic stress is referred to as a "disorder." You will note in my writing I limit the use of the term "disorder," preferring just post-traumatic stress. The reason is simple. Having tragic images stored in the mind is a very normal condition after participating in abnormal events. In fact, it is a good indication that the mind is functioning properly. Having those images recreated as a result of some type of trigger is normal too. Just as normal as seeing "four" in your head when asked what two plus two equals. The term "disorder" speaks to a greater level of unrest within a healthy mind, basically describing a strong mind that is on "overload." The good news is the disorder can be controlled through proper medical intervention so the resulting condition becomes post-traumatic stress "order," not "disorder." The bad news is this change cannot be accomplished overnight. There is no quick fix for post-traumatic stress disorder. I feel that fact deserves to be repeated. There is no quick fix for post-traumatic stress disorder. There are prescription drugs that can positively impact the condition and professional people who know how to prescribe them. These same highly qualified people can serve as guides to take someone from the "disorder" phase to the "order" stage of the affliction. I would suggest the worst legal drug, the one that will truly damage a healthy mind that is trying to deal with bad memories, is alcohol. Yes, alcohol is a drug, a depressant, and although it brings an instant feeling of relief, it will drive you deeper into depression and add more confusion to the chaos going on inside the brain. If you are having difficulty living with a past event, stay away from alcohol. This advice comes from someone who has witnessed many good people lose it all because of booze. The first thing to go was their significant other, along with their children, followed by their house, friends, some family members, and lastly their job. Some even lost their life. Approximately sixty-five percent of the victims of suicides I investigated, as well as those in which I intervened, were legally intoxicated. I know I mentioned that fact earlier, but this deserves repeating as well. While we are on the subject of alcohol I feel obligated to add that post-traumatic stress is similar to alcoholism in the sense that once you have it you have it for life. You either control it on your terms or it will control you. Bottom line, get used to living with it because it isn't going to disappear.

I also believe post-traumatic stress cannot be cured. The key to overcoming it is to understand that although it cannot be totally removed from the mind it can be effectively managed. P.T.S.D. is like having a scar on your leg that only you can see when you take off your slacks. Sure it's there, but you don't think about it until you change your clothes and look down. The key? Don't look down. Over-simplification perhaps, but the theory is applicable. Just as recovering alcoholics have to stay away from alcohol, those afflicted with post-traumatic stress must try to avoid triggers. Alcoholics in recovery share a common prayer, "God grant me the serenity to accept the things I cannot change, the courage to change the things I can, and the wisdom to know the difference." Regardless of religious affiliation this prayer applies to post-traumatic stress as well, for its message is very clear and right on target. Even for those who have lost sight of their God can live by these words, and use them to look deep into their inner self. Most of the time "what can be changed," and "what can't," are quite clear, the difficult part often evolves around "the wisdom to know the difference." Our minds never seem to stop, and although a bad thought may spoil the moment, a good one can make the day. The amount of time and effort it takes to produce either is about the same, the choice is ours.

Making that choice is directly related to not being able to use that delete key our minds never came equipped with. Instead we have the capacity to "cut" and "paste" whatever we want within our minds. During the course of my daily routine there were triggers that would bring back appalling images stored away within my trained investigative mind. I found that I could replace these images by looking at photographs of victims taken during happier times, before their deaths, when their faces radiated with smiles. Family photos contained within case files, those printed on the front page of the newspaper to show the good side of a bad story, or those taken for school pictures were key to bad image replacement. Not just by taking a casual glance, but also by actually studying the picture much the same as I would a crime scene photo, committing them to my memory. I trained my mind to cut and paste the good image of a specific person over the bad. Using this same mental image replacement technique I could if I wanted to, visualize three instead of four when asked what two plus two equaled. I found replacement of a bad mental representation with a good one was something within my power to do. The ability to sort, store, and select a better mental picture over a negative one is simply an image replacement for an unwanted representation, which when triggered, is not allowed to linger. I use this same methodology whenever the Gustafson family is triggered into my thought process. Instead of crime scene images I visualize them as they appeared in family photos. When they had smiles on their faces and were happy. Sean Coffey was a boy who loved to wander. I have a Norman Rockwell print hanging in my home of a boy dressed in jeans sitting on a garden fence watching a freight train going by off in the distance. Although his face is not specific you can sense the boy's wanderlust. I too was that boy many years ago. Whenever I pass through the intersection where Sean was killed I think of him, there is no way that I cannot. Instead of visualizing him lying in the roadway I think of the boy in the Rockwell print. Chelsea Adams remains a pretty two-year-old sound asleep all dressed up in her holiday outfit. Whenever I pass by the house where Kelci Fortunato was shot I think of her as she happily appeared in her high school yearbook in her band uniform, not unconscious on her back on her kitchen floor surrounded by the smell of gun smoke. I use this same method to influence other unwanted memories. This image replacement application took time to accomplish. I found by utilizing it I could manage my triggers rather than have them control me by bringing forth a fond predetermined image when hit with a bad trigger, or even better, when I knew one was coming. I grew to understand what I could change, what I couldn't, and the difference between the two. The choice was mine. When it comes to tragic loss we have within ourselves an ability to make the bad stuff take a back seat in our brain. Surely it takes practice, but doesn't anything we wish to get better at require the same?

Loss of sleep, low self-esteem, nightmares, repetitive bad dreams, work avoidance, panic attacks, and feeling disconnected with family, friends, and coworkers are warnings that things aren't right in the emergency work place. What many emergency workers who have symptoms of post-traumatic stress do not often understand is their brain isn't damaged, the human spirit within their mind is. For some people post-traumatic stress is something the other person has, or even worse, really doesn't even exist. Well guess what? It does and no one is immune.

I got into police work thinking I could make a difference for the better in the town where I grew up. I was raised within a religious doctrine that taught me to believe in the divine spirit. An invisible being that encompassed God in all his goodness and mercy. Oh how I believed, for the only other alternative was the devil, which existed without form or shape. Surely various artists have portrayed the devil in a variety of renditions, some abstract in form, existing in the spiritual world which in and of itself is hard to grasp hold of. The only time I felt I would come in contact with either would be when I died, and if I led a good life, God would certainly be the one I hoped to see. Ironically, I didn't have to wait until death to meet the devil, because I came face to face with him on more than one occasion. I saw him in the flesh, looked him in the eye, and even talked to him, not that I wanted to. For me the devil came in the form of evil beings that possessed cowardly destructive forces. Not just killers, but people, predominantly males, who for whatever reason felt they could hurt others without consequence. They came with ordinary names, but

WILLIAM MAY

Satan wasn't one of them even though there was evil within them.
Contrary to artistic belief, the devil is not red in color, nor does he
possess horns and a forked tail. The devil is human in appearance yet
subhuman in existence, easily mistaken in such clever disguise.

I am a Christian, although a poor example of one at best. I have
hardened in my religious beliefs with the passing of time. I remain
grateful that I did not have to walk in the shoes that made the
footprints my profession required me to follow. I witnessed firsthand
the true meaning of perseverance, which has made me a stronger
person. Yet through it all I cannot bring myself to forgive people who
intentionally hurt others. I refuse to. Forgiveness in this instance
fosters a connotation that intentional hurt is acceptable. Taken to the
extreme, forgiveness can lead to feelings of compassion for the one
who caused the damage. I reserve my compassion for those who
suffered, not those who caused it. Religious fundamental teaching
allows for forgiving the person without excusing the act. When it
comes to wantonly or recklessly taking the life of another, aggravated
assault, rape, and sexual abuse of a child, there is no room in my heart
or mind for forgiveness. Certainly those acts cannot be excused. Am I
angry? Am I bitter? No not really. I'm just the product of a criminal
justice system that preaches the doctrine of punishment, and in some
cases, rehabilitation, not forgiveness. There is also a part of me that is
concerned about recidivism. What message is delivered to people,
especially the young, when grave harm can be forgiven? The stronger
message should be severe accountability sent by our system of justice
and let God do what he does best with respect to forgiveness for those
responsible. I doubt God will forgive some of the evil people I came
in contact with. I guess that's why I believe in hell.

Unlike in my younger years, I now believe that heaven starts
when we arrive into this world, not when we depart it. I share in Andy
Gustafson's belief that our world is not more like heaven because of
our own choosing, not God's. Which relates directly to my previously
mentioned concept of living in a world built on the foundation of the
love of a child. Why can't we as adults, regardless of the gender,

religious belief, sexual orientation, color of skin, or political conviction be more caring toward one another? We have come a long way as a society but we still have a long journey ahead of us. Hurt is a four-letter word too, far worse than any to come out of any locker room. Why do some men, the term "men" deliberately expressed because they are our greatest offenders, feel they have exclusive license to violently hurt others? Certainly we can have an unintentional accident and either cause or suffer harm, but there should be no room in our society for intentional hurt. Causing harm to another person as a result of impaired operation of any vehicle whether it is by alcohol, drugs, electronic device usage, or other distraction is another form of inexcusable hurt. There is no excuse for such inconsideration of others.

I didn't know when I started out that police work would make me a different person. Midway through my career I moved out of my hometown simply because I needed a place where I could walk or ride without any bad triggers. Doing something good for someone else even without the expectation of a "thank you" took hold of me. Became something I practiced as often as I could, which became a rewarding mental experience, not just for me but the receiving party as well. Want to experience a fantastic feeling? The next time you attempt to park at a crowded mall and another vehicle arrives at the only parking spot at exactly the same time you do, wave the other person into the space. Another spot will open up very soon. When waging war against bad you have to have a powerful army of good on your side in order to win. I also took up friendships with people outside of my profession. I got away from the war stories. Nothing like being at a police cookout and having someone ask, "Do you remember the day so and so blew his brains out with a shot gun up on such an such street?" Of course I remembered it. How could I forget a flattened form of skin and hair that once was the three dimensional face of a person I knew? Over the last seven years of my retired life I have learned to play three different musical instruments so well I jam with ease when I get together with other musicians playing in public. I strongly recommend music as a diversion from unwanted thoughts. If not music, choose something you enjoy. Most important, something that makes your mind work out just like your body would on a treadmill.

Writing about interesting events that occurred during my career, especially the ones with happy endings, or those that brought me close to people of exceptional fortitude, is a great mental exercise for me. I would strongly recommend writing as a great way to ease the mind. Write about the "good stuff," the "good people" that came into your life. They're stored away in your center of consciousness. Want to feel good? Write about them! Write with purpose. Even documenting a tragic event in your own life, and what you did to help overcome it, might help someone else better cope with an unexpected difficult journey their mind never expected to take. If you have trouble finding a topic, write about yourself. You are, after all, unique. Your story is unlike any other. You are, whether you know it or not, special. Writing is therapeutic, good for the mind as well as the soul.

There seems to be a consensus that people are fragile, but in reality the human spirit, that inner will to survive, is very strong within each of us. I included a few examples earlier of people who clearly demonstrated this trait after being dealt horrific blows in their lives. I wanted to convey to my reader by way of extreme examples that life can maintain meaningful purpose regardless of how horrific a life experience might be. Each of the survivors mentioned here shared many of the common emotions felt after tragic loss: disbelief, anger, sorrow, depression, and even some guilt, though the latter undeserving. With the passing of time they reached various levels of acceptance, which is ongoing to this day. During their initial stages of trying to cope they demonstrated a need to put the broken pieces of their lives back together as best they could. There was a defining moment when they decided they had to fix themselves. Some told me the exact moment when this self-revelation occurred while others could not, but either way they each made a personal decision at some point to try and heal their minds, and on some occasions, their broken bodies as well. An undertaking of self-repair that took years to achieve, where over an extended period of time, their level of self-wellness reached acceptable levels. They found new purpose and in doing so became part of the solution rather than the problem. Andy Gustafson summed this up quite accurately when he told me one morning, "I had to get out of me and become a part of we." A powerful statement made by a man of great inner strength who could have, and almost did, let his life go, yet chose to become a better person by helping others. He became an important part of the "we," and did what children do best; he brought love into our world.

Each of the survivors I put forth as examples suffered severe post-traumatic stress as a result of a one-time event. One found his family murdered within their home. At the age of nine a girl witnessed her brother killed. Another barely survived after being shot in the head, while yet another bathed and dressed her two-year old deccased daughter desperately not wanting to let her go. Unlike the emergency responder, these people were first party to the devastation. They lived through the nightmare and struggled during the months that followed. Over time they grew to understand there was nothing they could do to change what had happened. They will tell you that the pain of their experiences took to them down to levels of despair far beyond anything they could imagine. They all carry with them horrible memories that can be triggered back to the forefront of their minds when least expected. They will tell you that the passing of time does help. Doesn't make the pain go completely away; just helps. As Suzanne Coffey Camacho told me during our collaboration while writing the chapter about her brother, "time soothes." I would suggest in those instances where the "this too shall pass" of your life cannot exist, "time soothes" can thrive.

Surely every crisis is different, but emergency workers can take meaningful purpose from within the devastation they witness firsthand. As a group they cannot always prevent the devastation they are required to work within, but they can help correct it. They can bring hope and comfort to those in desperate need. They can learn from those who survive by observing the courage put forth. They can become a part of that "we." Certainly there is entitlement to feelings of disbelief, sorrow, grief, anger, and even guilt. Some can be extreme. These thoughts are very normal when working in an arena of human abnormalities. If you are about to embark on a career in emergency services be aware of this. You might be told that all you need is "thick skin." Not so, rubber gloves and protective clothing come with the job. You will be trained precisely on how to react to crisis, but not much time will be spent on how to manage depressing thoughts that come long after the devastation is over, although they deserve equal consideration before the fact, not after.

One question a new emergency service recruit might want to ask during their initial employment interview, "What does your agency do with respect to managing post-traumatic stress?" Do not be mistaken; my intent is not to discourage anyone from seeking a rewarding career in emergency services. Based on my experience there is no greater calling than that of helping others, especially those in desperate need. Although working within the various emergency service professions can be stressful, not everyone develops post-traumatic stress disorder as a result. The best estimate is approximately thirty percent do. Much depends on where you work, what you're required to do, what you encounter, aspects of your personality, your genetic profile, your body chemistry, and a host of other factors. There are personality tests available that can tell you if you are susceptible, but no test exists to predict absolute immunity. As such, it is far better to have a good understanding of what you are getting yourself into and have a plan in place in the event P.T.S.D. comes knocking on your door, or that of a coworker. Preparation starts by understanding the various characteristics of the disorder. The more you know about how your mind can be impacted the easier it will be to pick yourself up if you ever take the fall.

If you are already working in the emergency services field and feel apprehensive about your job, remind yourself that you are only human. Regardless of your faith, there are powers much stronger than any skill you possess that often determine the outcome of an event. One key factor that must be understood regardless of individual discipline or level of expertise is that often, very often, no matter how well an emergency response is conducted, the end result can be severe. Death and serious injury do not settle well within the mind regardless of circumstance. Nor does failure, which is often falsely perceived. If there are no programs within your organization, such as post-incident stress debriefings or one-on-one counseling, request they be put in place. The mind can be a difficult thing to put back together once it is broken. Mending an occasional crack is far easier than trying to pick up all the broken pieces. When faced with troubled thoughts I would recommend removing yourself from the "me" of your life and join the "we" of the world. Not necessarily the "we" of your chosen profession, but the "we" of the world. I would also hold close to the premise that "time soothes." Harboring depressing thoughts within your mind is not healthy. The most important thing you can do is to get those feelings out. Talk about them with someone in the medical profession you can trust. Someone far enough removed from your personal self to allow for objective thinking to prevail.

What you have just read represents a sorting of some of my thoughts and arranging them in the chronological order in which they occurred. Not hard to do, really, when actual dates apply. What was difficult early on in my career was sorting out the particulars of each event so that bad recollections formed the foundation on which good thoughts were built. I wanted to show via manuscript how the mind can be effectively controlled. To provide the reader with something that can be physically held, hopefully understood, and in doing so, put a face and body to post-traumatic stress disorder that is so difficult to visualize. The only mind we are allowed to wander around is our own, and I felt it might help if you were given the opportunity to roam around mine. This is not so much a "self-help book" as it is a "what I did" synopsis. We are all different. When it comes to receiving and processing shock and awe some people are more sensitive than others.

What worked for me may not necessarily work for you. Post-traumatic stress is a serious affliction. In acute cases it can be deadly. If you work in emergency services and you haven't felt right about what you do on a daily basis you may suffer from fatigue or maybe post-traumatic stress. Both are very real conditions, which if not tended to properly can take their toll. If you suffer from either there are people in professions readily available to help you. They will find what works best for you until you can understand what is going on and manage your condition on your own. Most health insurance programs cover the cost. Don't be afraid to inquire. Don't wait too long to ask. In this instance time is not on your side, nor is drug or alcohol consumption.

What about my heavy glass hypothesis? What about using your mental "cut" and "paste" keys in place of the "delete" key your mind never came with? How about the brain to balloon comparison? Kind of stretching it I guess, but each are capable of expansion and both start with the letter "B." I know all of this is not medical science by any stretch of the imagination, but I warned you. I'm just an old cop using a simple approach to help manage a very complex problem that exists in the real world of emergency services. I tried to provide an overall view of what works for me. Notice I used the present tense of the word "work." I did that because I do not have post-traumatic stress disorder. Haven't since 1991. I do however have a condition known as post-traumatic stress "order;" P.T.S.O. You won't find this condition listed anywhere else other than in this book because I developed it by using mental image replacement. I'll be in this healthy state the rest of my life. I can think of far worse places for my mind to be. Plus I enjoy that word "order," especially as I grow older. The dictionary defines order as, "a situation in which everything is in its correct place; a state of peace and obedience to law." Now that's healthy. I like that.

I go back to my hometown upon occasion. Went this past year late one evening during the holiday season. There wasn't any snow on the ground as is often the case in late December, but even without it there was a certain tranquility around the Town Common. As I stood there in the darkness I thought about the thousands of people, young and old alike, who had walked upon the grassy common floor over the years just as I had. Maybe sat for a moment and listened to a band concert on Thursday nights during the summer, accompanied by the laughter of children spirited on by the music. Good people. Hard working people. People that care about their neighbor; one another. On this night only quiet filled the cold night air. An occasional vehicle passed by intruding upon the stillness, interrupting my moment of peaceful reconciliation. Perhaps it was the three churches that surrounded me, all of different faiths but common in their belief that good overcomes evil, that gave me such an inner feeling of serenity. Maybe it was the passing of time and events that stood with me, beside me. Hanging on for whatever meaning or purpose, not wanting to let go, nor should they. They are what they were. They are what I am. Or was it the season that made me feel the tranquility surrounding me? How great it was, and is, to be free of disturbance, to know the true meaning of peace. I walked across the common under a bright moonlit sky, down Highland Street, and onto 7th Avenue at the Hillside Cemetery, passing the grave markers that line both sides. Some names engraved upon them more meaningful to me than others, yet all known to me. I looked to each as the people they once were, not what they could have been, or what put them in the ground I was standing upon. I prefer to think that the only thing that can be done for the dead is to bury them, pray for them, remember them with love, and when necessary, give their survivors the justice they deserve. There is, however, so much we can do for the living, for one another. We can get out of ourselves and care for others. At the very least we can ask, "How are you doing?" On some occasions nothing has to be said, just a hug will do.

While standing upon my hallowed ground my thoughts drifted back thirty-seven years to the elderly man who had lost his wallet at the telephone booth in West Townsend in November 1975. When a firefighter found it and I returned it to him. When he said, "You know, I've heard stories about how people in small towns take care of others in need. How they look out for one another. I never expected so many would show up to help me find my wallet. I don't even live here and look at all the people who came out to help. This would never have happened in the city. I can't believe it. I just can't believe it." Well maybe he shouldn't have, because those who showed up that night came to fight a fire not find a lost wallet. Yet I know if I had requested assistance to find that wallet on that night so long ago the same people would have showed up to help. No I'm not the village Indian Chief that Dr. Polizoti had suggested I couldn't be. I'm just a retired small town Police Chief, who on this night, was standing among "his people."

In an attempt to bring greater awareness to the emotional stress emergency workers encounter and the negative impact post-traumatic stress can have on those who face trauma on a day-to-day basis, I ask that once you have read this book to go online (i.e. Amazon.com, Goodreads.com, Barnesandnoble.com, or any web source relevant to the subject matter) and post your review. Hopefully, by working together, we can provide greater awareness and support for those who are so negatively impacted by this condition while working as emergency care providers.

Thanks,
William May

CPSIA information can be obtained at www.ICGtesting.com
Printed in the USA
BVOW01s2015070814

361874BV00003B/608/P

9 780988 316201